92⁵⁰

D0380264

User-Centred Library Websites

CHANDOS
INFORMATION PROFESSIONAL SERIES

Series Editor: Ruth Rikowski
(email: Rikowskigr@aol.com)

Chandos' new series of books are aimed at the busy information professional. They have been specially commissioned to provide the reader with an authoritative view of current thinking. They are designed to provide easy-to-read and (most importantly) practical coverage of topics that are of interest to librarians and other information professionals. If you would like a full listing of current and forthcoming titles, please visit our web site **www.chandospublishing.com** or contact Hannah Grace-Williams on email info@chandospublishing.com or telephone number +44 (0) 1993 848726.

New authors: we are always pleased to receive ideas for new titles; if you would like to write a book for Chandos, please contact Dr Glyn Jones on email gjones@chandospublishing.com or telephone number +44 (0) 1993 848726.

Bulk orders: some organisations buy a number of copies of our books. If you are interested in doing this, we would be pleased to discuss a discount. Please contact Hannah Grace-Williams on email info@chandospublishing.com or telephone number +44 (0) 1993 848726.

User-Centred Library Websites

Usability evaluation methods

CAROLE A. GEORGE

RETIRÉ DE LA COLLECTION UNIVERSELLE
Bibliothèque et Archives nationales du Québec

Chandos Publishing
Oxford · England

Chandos Publishing (Oxford) Limited
TBAC Business Centre
Avenue 4
Station Lane
Witney
Oxford OX28 4BN
UK
Tel: +44 (0) 1993 848726 Fax: +44 (0) 1865 884448
Email: info@chandospublishing.com
www.chandospublishing.com

First published in Great Britain in 2008

ISBN:
978 1 84334 359 2 (paperback)
978 1 84334 360 8 (hardback)
1 84334 359 2 (paperback)
1 84334 360 6 (hardback)

© Carole A. George

British Library Cataloguing-in-Publication Data.
A catalogue record for this book is available from the British Library.

All rights reserved. No part of this publication may be reproduced, stored in or introduced into a retrieval system, or transmitted, in any form, or by any means (electronic, mechanical, photocopying, recording or otherwise) without the prior written permission of the Publishers. This publication may not be lent, resold, hired out or otherwise disposed of by way of trade in any form of binding or cover other than that in which it is published without the prior consent of the Publishers. Any person who does any unauthorised act in relation to this publication may be liable to criminal prosecution and civil claims for damages.

The Publishers make no representation, express or implied, with regard to the accuracy of the information contained in this publication and cannot accept any legal responsibility or liability for any errors or omissions.

The material contained in this publication constitutes general guidelines only and does not represent to be advice on any particular matter. No reader or purchaser should act on the basis of material contained in this publication without first taking professional advice appropriate to their particular circumstances.

Typeset by Avocet Typeset, Chilton, Aylesbury, Bucks.
Printed in the UK and USA.

Contents

Contents

List of figures and tables

Figures

Tables

About the author

Carole A. George is a human factors researcher with the Carnegie Mellon University Libraries. She joined the University Library in 2000. With an emphasis on improving users' access to information, Ms George's work focuses on usability studies of library websites and evaluation studies of library services. Her research interests and efforts have been directed towards user-centred interface evaluation and information behaviour studies.

Her work in usability studies at the university emphasises the need to involve users in design and development activities and hear what they have to say. Despite all best efforts at detecting usability problems based on guidelines, usability specialists need to rely on users' feedback as it relates to designing a user-centred website. Ms George strives to provide information that informs the development of user-centred libraries, thus making finding and using libraries' information resources and services easier, ultimately encouraging the use of information that supports academic as well as nonacademic endeavours.

Previously, Ms George was a research associate at the Learning Research and Development Center at the University of Pittsburgh. She holds a M.Ed. in Research Methodology and Evaluation and an Ed.D. in Administrative and Policy Studies.

The author may be contacted at:
E-mail: *cgeorge@andrew.cmu.edu*

Preface

More frequently than ever before, students, faculty and others are accessing the resources of college and university libraries using the library's website. For that reason it is of immediate importance to be certain that the website and other digital interfaces or website pages are easy to use and understand by the users. This is referred to as a user-centred website. Involving users in the process of website design and development is the best method of ensuring that the website is user-centred.

This book covers methods that can be used to gather feedback from users of your website about the organisation, navigation, terminology and general usability of a website. This book is a guide to usability evaluation techniques that are employed to design a user-centred website.

This book will guide you through the usability evaluation methods from the early stages of design to the late stages of testing a finished website. It will help you to determine which evaluation method will provide you with the best feedback at every stage of the development and design or redesign cycle of your website. It will help you to understand the evaluation methods, prepare for the session, recruit participants, facilitate the session, analyse the results, and write the report. With feedback from the targeted users, you will learn whether they can understand your terminology, navigate your site, and find the information that you provide.

Examples are provided to help you with the letters, e-mails, forms and questionnaires that you might need. By involving the target users in the development and evaluation of your website throughout the design and development cycle, you will be better prepared to design a user-centred website that your users will continue to use to access your information resources.

What is user-centred design?

To begin with, think about the website as having a back-end and a front-end. The back-end of the website is not visible to the end-users, the primary target users (students, faculty and others) who are trying to find information and complete tasks using the library website. The back-end includes the information, resources and functionality offered by the website – such things as the scholarly databases, the library catalogue, and the software that enables functionality, such as simple and advanced searching of the library catalogue and searching special collection documents by words or phrases.

The front-end, the website end-user interface, is what is visible to the people using the website. It might be what many think of as the website. The front-end includes such things as screen displays, font sizes and colour, the terminology, the primary and secondary navigation (the links to the main features and pages of the website), and the simple and advanced search pages. As shown in Figure 1.1, the front-end is designed to collect information from the end-user and process the information in order to access the back-end components.

User-centred design often refers to the design and usability of the front-end of the website – the end-user

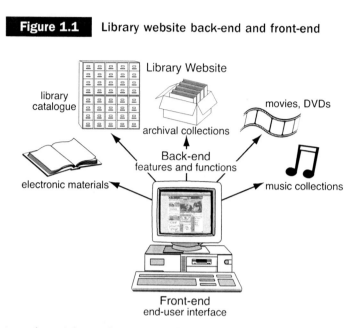

Figure 1.1 Library website back-end and front-end

interface. The end-user interface is the link between the end-user and the features and functionality offered by the website in the back-end. This book is about creating a user-centred, easy to use, website design by collecting information from representative users and other stakeholders with evaluation methods and techniques. This book will describe the various techniques that will enable you to create the easy-to-use website.

User-centred design

> If a gadget isn't easy to use, then just get rid of it! (Carey, 2007)

While the comedian Drew Carey might not be an expert in product and system design, his views about product use mirror those of typical users. Products, gadgets, systems and websites need to be easy to operate and useful if people are to continue to use them. And it is the target users who determine what is easy. This is why products and systems need to be user-centred, that is, designed with the user in mind. This chapter describes user-centred design and its relationship to university and college library websites.

Simply stated, user-centred design refers to how easy a product, website or computer-based system is to use based on the users' perceptions. Sometimes referred to as usability, user-friendliness or usability engineering, user-centred design is a relatively new approach to the focus of website design. The process of designing user-centred products focuses on the needs of users and the design of technology to serve users (Norman, 1998). At the core, user-centred design focuses on the usability or ease of use of the product or system.

In the early 1980s, the design of products and systems began to focus more on people's ability to use products easily, and when using interactive systems, to complete tasks that would serve their needs. User-centred design puts the users first. Wesley E. Woodson, in an early book on human factors design, defines human factors engineering, a method of developing a user-centred design, as:

> ...the practice of designing products so that users can perform required use, operation, service, and supportive tasks with a minimum of stress and maximum of efficiency. To accomplish this, the designer must understand and acknowledge the needs, characteristics, capabilities, and limitations of the intended user and design from the human out, making the design fit the user instead of forcing the user to fit the design. (Woodson, 1981: vii)

Later in the 1980s, in an early introduction to human–computer interaction, after observing how humans interact with computer-based systems, Paul A. Booth described user-centred design as:

> Any system designed for people to use should be easy to learn (and remember), useful, that is, contain functions people really need in their work, and be easy and pleasant to use. (Booth, 1989: 300)

Patrick W. Jordan, in *An Introduction to Human-Computer Interaction*, agrees that the design needs to consider the ease-of-use of products. He describes usability by saying:

> Informally, usability issues can be thought of as pertaining to how easy a product is to use, i.e., they are to do with the 'user-friendliness' of products. (Jordan 1998: 5)

Joseph S. Dumas and Janice C. Redish, in *A Practical Guide to Usability Testing*, simply say that:

> Usability means that the *people who use the product* can do so *quickly and easily* to accomplish *their own* tasks. (Dumas and Redish 1999: 4)

All agree that a user-centred design focuses on how easily end-users, those for whom the website is targeted for use, can accomplish their tasks. For library websites, the primary end-users are typically the students, faculty and employees of the university or school. End-users determine the usability of the website based on their perception of the product's quality, ease of use, ease of learning and relearning, the product's intuitiveness, and the users' appreciation of the usefulness of the product (Barnum 2002: 6). 'People consider a product "easy to learn and use" in terms of the *time* it takes to do what they want, the number of *steps* they go through and the *success* they have in predicting the right action to take' (Booth 1989: 5).

While a user-centred website is easy to use and useful for end-users, it might require some work and extra effort to design. To better understand and create a user-centred website, consider the following factors that have been associated with user-centred products and websites (Booth 1989: 5; Jordan 1998: 12–13; Neilsen 2003a):

- *Learnability*: The basics of the product are easy to learn or relearn; first-time or novice users can accomplish basic tasks within reasonable time limits the first time they encounter the design.

- *Effectiveness* (ease of use): The product is easy to use within reasonable time limits and error rates.

- *Efficiency*: Once users have learned the design, they will perform the tasks quickly and at a high level; this is an important component for a product that will be used frequently and repeatedly.

- *Memorability*: This refers to how easy the product is for users who return after a period of inactivity; this is important for products that are used infrequently or after fairly long absences.

- *Attitude, satisfaction*: The product meets the needs as perceived by the users; the design is pleasant and appealing.

- *Errors*: These describe the number of errors users make, the severity of the errors, and how easily users can recover from the errors; a user-centred design limits the number and severity of users' errors.

- *Usefulness*: This describes how adequately the system supports the range of tasks that it was designed to support; the ability of the system to do what users need it to do; users' ability to complete tasks that meet their objectives and expectations.

Gitte Lindgaard (1994: 20, 38) describes other common characteristics of usable systems: the navigation takes the reader through the page of the interface, the website, and home again; the terminology is common to the targeted users; the design is consistent with users' expectations; information-rich sites are designed for readability; and the appearance is pleasing.

Why design a user-centred website?

Workplaces, including university and college libraries, have made tremendous changes in how they conduct their work. Jordan asserts that:

> Nearly all professional jobs now involve the use of computers. This has meant that over the last few years entire workforces have had to become 'computer-literate' or rather that computers have had to become 'user-friendly'. (Jordan, 1998: 2)

His statement is appropriate in today's university and college libraries now that they are offering a great deal of their services and collections through a library website or other digital sites. The usability of the website is of immediate importance. The major reason to design a user-centred library website is to make it easier for users to access the vast amount of information, to a great extent scholarly, provided by libraries through their websites. As the usability of a website increases, it is reasonable to conclude that users' access to the website and consequently their use of scholarly information will increase.

If the website is easy to use and the information is useful, easy to find, download, save or print, users are more likely to continue to use the website and return. If the information is hard to find or users get lost in the middle of the website, they will seek information elsewhere. If they encounter obstacles or become frustrated, they will leave the website. If libraries want people to access their online resources, it becomes their responsibility and a priority to provide their resources in a user-centred environment. Libraries first need to understand their targeted users and the changing user population.

Changing needs in the end-user population

As Jeffery Rubin describes, in the early years of software development:

> users of computer-based products were 'hackers,' possessing expert knowledge of computers and mechanical devices, a love of technology, the desire to tinker, and pride in their ability to troubleshoot and repair any problem. (Rubin, 1994: 5–9)

Because the primary users of early software were not only knowledgeable, but enjoyed responding to software problems, products were developed for the technically savvy user.

As end-user groups began to change and become more diverse and less technically skilled, the design and development of interactive systems began to change. The emphasis on the design of interactive systems began to focus on the usability of the system, that is, the ease of learning and of using, and the satisfaction of users as they interacted with the system (Rosson and Carroll, 2001: 9). Today's users are even more diverse. Many, if not most, have few technical skills and do not enjoy tinkering and learning the system. The challenge for designers is obvious, and the focus of application development is on ease of use for the end-user.

The work of cognitive scientists who have studied the learning challenges faced by users has affected the design of interactive systems (Rosson and Carroll 2001: 12–13). Based on their studies, cognitive scientists have suggested that learning requires users to connect their task needs with the application services. The research indicates that new users rely on previous knowledge of activities and objects to understand how to complete their tasks using the application. The research also suggests that information from targeted users about the usability of the application is relevant throughout the development cycle in an iterative development process. Thus, the first step in designing systems based on users' needs is to learn more about users.

End-user population

Understanding the user population is essential to the development of a user-centred system. In *Crossing the Chasm*, Geoffrey A. Moore (1991: 11–13), describes five groups of users attracted to a new technology product:

- *Innovators* (very small group): Technologists who are eager for new high-tech products, sometimes seeking out new advancements and products even before the formal launch. Though a small group, they are important because their endorsement is reassuring to the other groups of users.

- *Early adopters* (small group): Though not technologists, they are eager to accept the benefits of new technology and buy into new product concepts early. They rely on their own intuition and vision to imagine the usefulness of the product in making buying decisions.

- *The early majority* (about one-third): Though similar to early adopters in the way they relate to technology, they are also practical. Knowing many new technologies end up as passing fads, they wait to see how the product performs with other people before investing.

- *The late majority* (about one-third): While sharing many concerns of the early majority, they are different in that they are not comfortable with new technology. Before investing in the product, they wait until it is an established standard and look for lots of support.

- *Laggards* (small group): This group is comprised of people who want nothing to do with technology. They will buy into technology when is it buried into another product or when it is necessary in order to perform their jobs.

How can libraries create user-centred websites?

For libraries to create user-centred websites, in addition to understanding the user population, they need to be aware of the principles of user-centred design. There are three principles to describe the process of creating a user-centred design. These were first proposed by John D. Gould and Clayton Lewis (1985: 300) and are still in use today:

- Focus early and continuously on users and their tasks. Before beginning the design process, determine the characteristics of the targeted user population, their objectives and their priorities.

- Early in the development, use evaluation methods to observe, record, and analyse users' performance when using simulations or prototypes of the website in various stages of the development.

- Use an iterative design process, that is, develop the website using a cycle of design, test and redesign. Use this process throughout the design.

Briefly stated, to create a user-centred design, focus early on users, employ evaluation procedures continuously within an iterative process of design, test and redesign. These are explored in more detail below.

Focus early and continuously on users and their tasks

> From the moment you know enough to talk about a product – any product, whether it's hardware, software, games, or Web pages – you know too much to be able to tell if the product would be usable for a human being who doesn't know what you know. (Barnum, 2002: xiii)

Involving targeted users of the website, representatives of the primary end-user groups, in the early stages of the design and throughout the development of the website is necessary to provide the end-user's perspective on how they use and value the website (Torres, 2002: 223). When this effort begins in the early stages of development, changes are easier and involve less time for developers. Involving users only towards the end of the development cycle, after usability testing of a finished product, can result in major changes in the product's design that are time-consuming and expensive. Because of the expense and time required, it can be too late to respond to major changes. For the best results, usability evaluation that involves representative users is an ongoing process starting early and continuing throughout the development cycle.

'Designing successful products depends upon knowing about users' behaviour as well as their preferences' (Tec-Ed Services, 2008a). Designers and developers know too much about the product to be objective about the usability. Although involving all stakeholders, such as developers, designers, content experts and usability personnel, throughout the development provides an opportunity to learn about their unique perspectives, to create a user-centred design, the focus must be on the potential users and their behaviour as they interact with the system

In his book, *Don't Make Me Think! A Common Sense Approach to Web Usability*, Steve Krug (2000: 21–9) describes how people use websites:

- *People don't read they scan*: Though we might like to believe that people who visit websites thoughtfully peruse the page and then choose what best meets their needs, according to Krug, they actually just scan the page looking for words or phrases. Krug suggests that people scan pages because they are in a hurry and know that they don't need most of what is on the page. With their experience reading newspapers, magazines and books, people have become good at scanning.

- *People don't make optimal choices, they 'satisfice'*: Knowing that people scan website pages, we tend to think that they scan the entire page, think about what choices make the most sense to achieve objectives, and then they select the best choice. Instead, end-users scan only parts of the page and select choices that seem reasonable. Krug suggests that users do not have the time to read entire pages; that guessing is not penalised, is more fun, and is faster; and that weighing options may not lead to the best selections on poorly designed sites.

- *People muddle through*: Most people really do not understand how websites work. They seldom read instructions and just take their chances at trying to figure out how to use the website. Krug points out that this is true of both novice and experienced users. He suggests that how websites work is simply not very important to users. Once they find a method that works for them, they use it whether or not it is the best method. Users' choices might be surprising to developers who have taken a great deal of time to design a website that is logical to use, only to have users select what developers might consider illogical choices.

To learn more about users and their needs, start with a user needs assessment, watch users as they complete tasks using a prototype (a draft copy) of the website, the actual website, or a similar website. Examine other similar websites and how they satisfy users' needs (Norman, 1998). Based on the user needs analysis, construct prototypes and begin the cycle of iterative design, test, redesign and retest until the website meets the needs of the users determined by usability testing and usability standards. Focus on the end-users.

Early and throughout the process carry out usability evaluation methods

Usability evaluation is employing quantitative (empirical) and qualitative (non-empirical) methods to collect data that describe the usability of the website – how easy it is to learn, use, remember, recover from errors – to determine how pleasing and useful it is to the users. The collected data are used to further refine the website usability. Usability evaluation methods produce both quantitative and qualitative data. Some methods, such as think aloud protocols, produce both quantitative (e.g. error rates and completion time) and qualitative data (e.g. verbal reports and observations).

Empirical methods of evaluation, based on observations and measurements, produce quantitative data. You can collect quantitative data using methods such as think aloud protocols, contextual inquiry, surveys and attitude scales. In these methods the data can be observed and measured, and by using a form of quantitative analysis, result in information that can be used as benchmark data.

Benchmarks include empirical measures such as completion rates, error rates, completion time and attitude measures such as how users feel about the ease of use or the appearance of the end-user interface. In an iterative design process, benchmarks are a means of comparing system revisions over time and help indicate whether design changes have successfully addressed the issues or problems found in usability testing.

For example, when using an iterative design process in the development of the website, you can design a website prototype and then test for usability with representative users. Based on their feedback and your observations, you can refine the website and address found problems and issues and then retest. By comparing quantitative measures, you can determine whether your changes have successfully addressed previously found problems or issues.

Non-empirical methods of evaluation produce qualitative data. In usability evaluation, non-empirical methods are based on an inspection of the system which is compared with accepted usability standards or experts' knowledge of standards. When comparisons fail to meet usability standards, usability issues are detected. In usability inspection methods such as heuristic evaluation, expert reviews and cognitive walkthroughs, experts examine the interface from a user's point of view, looking for usability problems in order to refine the system. Usability inspection methods do not involve representative users. They rely on the reviewers' knowledge and experience.

In addition, participants' verbal responses collected during think aloud protocols, interviews and focus groups produce non-empirical, qualitative data. When these methods are conducted after users' interaction with a prototype or an existing website, users can provide feedback about usability problems and possible solutions. Non-empirical, qualitative data are useful for finding solutions to usability problems. 'Although quantitative data is required to accurately assess the usability of a system, it is the qualitative information that informs designers how to change an unusable system' (Booth, 1989: 128).

Jordan (1998: 81–4) suggests several methods for conducting usability evaluation on existing and proposed websites:

- *Benchmark existing products* before revising the product or creating a new product to evaluate current usability problems and provide a baseline for comparison of revised or new products.

- *Capture requirements*, such as user characteristics and product specifications, based on users' and other stakeholders' goals and objectives, to plan and design an early prototype.

- *Evaluate initial concepts* and prototypes early in product design; test several designs to determine direction and priorities in design and functionality.

- *Develop a concept* based on the previous step and use interactive prototypes to gain users' reactions and recommendations towards refining the website design.

- *Test the design* of a fully functional prototype in order to detect usability problems late in the product development cycle. While this might be too late to make major changes before release, the information can be used for minor changes and future products.

- *Evaluate the finished product* to determine usability issues after the release of the product. Because major changes at this late stage are not practical, found usability issues can be addressed in future designs. Additionally, results can be used for benchmarking data when compared with future designs to indicate product improvements.

Early in website development, use methods such as surveys, interviews or focus groups to complete a needs assessment to gather information from stakeholders and potential users. This information can feed the design of the website. Participatory design methods such as group interviews (focus groups), affinity diagrams, card sorting or paper prototyping involve stakeholders and potential users in the design process. Expert reviews, like heuristic evaluation, help to evaluate the website at any point in the design stages and early in the cycle to provide a means of identifying major problems early. Usability testing throughout the process helps in the collection of usability data.

Use an iterative design process throughout the design cycle

> It's impossible to produce a system that is completely right the first time round, so you must be ready to change. (Lindgaard, 1994: 33)

The idea of following usability and design guidelines to create a user-centred website without using evaluation methods is enticing though unrealistic. Unless the system is evaluated with potential users, developers cannot know if the website is user-centred and useful. The process of usability evaluation identifies usability problems with the website design. Following the evaluation, identified usability issues are addressed and the website is refined. 'The most important step in any usability evaluation is to go back and fix the problems that were identified' (Brinck, Gergle and Wood, 2002: 407). However, the process is not yet complete. You need to retest to determine if the usability issues have been successfully addressed.

Depending on the depth and complexity of the website, website development can include many rounds of design, testing and redesign. This type of development cycle is referred to as iterative design. Iterative design is a cyclical process that starts early in the development cycle and continues until the design of the interface is completed. It is a cycle of design, evaluation, redesign and evaluation, continuing until the interface is completed and meets users' needs and accepted standards for a user-centred design.

Conduct usability testing to detect problems and issues

Booth reminds us that during the early years of software development, products were designed for the designers and the developers themselves, as they were the primary users of the systems. He continues by saying:

> As designers are no longer typical of most users, we need tools, techniques, design practices and methodologies that will inform design and development teams of how users behave at an interface and what users require from a system. (Booth, 1989: 3)

Usability testing is a method that provides information about how users interact with a product or system. The findings are used to determine changes to the website in order to increase the website's usability. A frequently used method of usability testing is the think aloud protocol. Usability testing differs from other evaluation methods in the following ways (Nielsen, 1993: 165; Rubin, 1994: 25; Dumas and Redish, 1999: 22; Barnum, 2002: 9):

- The process involves real users from the target population of users (the primary users of the system).
- The users interact with the system by completing real tasks, i.e. tasks that they will likely attempt when using the completed system.
- The process involves observation and measurement of participants' behaviour and recordings of verbalisations of their responses to issues they encounter when using the system.

Usability testing with think aloud protocols is a quantitative as well as qualitative method of evaluation that uses observations and measurement to evaluate the usability of the interface or website, and verbal responses to collect usability information that is useful in refining the website. In contrast to other evaluation methods that use inspection or survey to collect information about the website, usability testing always involves representative users and produces information about how they interact with the actual website or a working prototype. 'Many systems have been developed that are considered to be functionally excellent, but perform badly in the real world' (Booth, 1989: 2). Thus, the best method of determining how the system will perform is to observe representative users completing real-world tasks.

Why is usability testing necessary?

If you follow usability guidelines when designing your system within an iterative design process, you might wonder why usability testing is necessary. However, despite all efforts to create a usable product, you can never be sure how users will interact with the working interface until you observe their behaviour (Lindgaard, 1994: 22). For this reason testing is essential. Users often do not respond in a logical manner, but can be distracted by their own objectives for accessing the website. Rather than peruse the website and check out all options, they quickly scan and choose what looks like the most direct option for their purposes.

Therefore, the design and evaluation of a website interface based solely on evaluation methods that do not involve users interacting with a functional website will not provide the feedback necessary to design a user-centred interface. The best way to determine if the website is usable is to evaluate the functional website by conducting usability testing with think aloud protocols. Think aloud protocols can be completed with representative users to collect usability data about how users interact with the website interface.

Usability testing with think aloud protocols does not replace other methods of evaluation, nor is it the final layer of the development cycle. Usability testing that comes late in the development cycle can be too late to address major usability defects. Fixing problems late in development can be time-consuming and expensive. Rather, usability testing is effective when used as one method of evaluation in an iterative design cycle. 'For tests to be effective, they must begin when the project starts and continue throughout the design/development process in test-modify-retest cycles' (Lindgaard, 1994: 27).

How do I interpret the results?

> It's true, the trickiest part of usability testing is making sure you draw the right conclusions from what you see. (Krug, 2000: 145)

Though interpreting the results of usability testing can be difficult, if not the most difficult part of the process, thinking about the results as they impact main categories of website design will help you to produce beneficial interpretations. Usability testing reveals problems and issues that generally fall into the categories described below (Krug, 2000: 31–2; Nielsen, 2000: 100–1, 2001a).

Navigation

Navigation, when referring to a website, is how easily users move through the system and understand where they are and how to return to previously viewed pages. Navigation issues also include issues related to error messages and how easily users recover from errors.

Jakob Nielsen (2001a) offers some tips for designing website navigation:

- There is no need to mention all the features of your website on every page; choose the main features and link to those. Providing a link to the homepage will put users just a click away from the basic features.

- Many people will use the search feature to find pages, thus will not know the website structure leading to the page they are on. Provide some structural links to the higher levels so that people have a better idea of where they are in the website structure.

- Local links that are related to the page content are helpful.

- Design a website structure from the users' perspective, rather than from the developers' perspective so the layout of the website will make better sense to users.

Screen design and layout

Screen design and layout concern the appearance of the screen displays and how information is presented. Good screen display includes information that is chunked into short blocks of text; headings that support scanning; font size, type and colour that are easily read; and presentation that uses high contrast of background and characters. Good screen display enables scanning for important information clues.

Look for problems, including too much text with too little white space – where the text is displayed in long paragraphs and pages. Look for headings that are difficult to find or important links that are embedded within the text.

> When writing for the Web, you're not only affecting the content, you're affecting the core user experience because users look at the text and the headlines first. (Nielsen, 2000: 100–1)

Writing for the web is very different than writing for the printed page. Nielsen (2000: 100–15) suggests the three main guidelines for writing for the web:

- *Write succinctly and keep text short*: When writing for the web use no more than 50 per cent of the words that would be used in printed text on navigation pages (pages that will take you to your destination page). The exception is when arriving at the destination if the page is a reprint of an article or paper.

- *Write for scanability*: To aid users' movement through the website, use two or even three levels of headers on pages. Use meaningful headers rather than 'cute', bulleted lists, and colour for emphasis. Write short paragraphs using plain language, beginning the page with the most important information because people will choose the first relevant choice. Write one idea per paragraph using a simple sentence structure. Use humour cautiously and with a light touch.

- *Use hypertext*: Hypertext can be used to split up long pages of information into shorter pages. Long pages of information can be intimidating to users. Rather than lose the depth of content, split the pages into chunks of information using hypertext to link the pages. Though users will scroll on the final destination pages, keep navigation pages short.

Terminology

Terminology concerns the words, sentences and abbreviations that are used on the website. Look for problems with words that are inconsistent with the user's terminology; use of jargon; and lack of clarity for text, headings, link names and labels.

Feedback

Feedback concerns the system's response to such things as errors or error warnings, messages, such as when files will be deleted, and how the system responds after users initiate an action. Look for problems with error recovery, slow response time, and feedback failing to alert users to what is happening.

Consistency

Consistency is the degree to which the system performs in a predictable manner throughout the website. Consistency is important in the display of information, the presentation of navigational links, the presentation of menu screens, the use of colour, and the display of exits. Consistency throughout the system improves learnability and helps users develop a sense of place, that is, to know where they are and how to move through the system.

Modality

Modality refers to the state of the system. With some applications, users need to enter a different mode, such as an 'edit' mode. Look for problems when changing modes.

Redundancies

Redundancies are repetitions throughout the system. These are problems when they are unnecessary and they interfere with users' actions. Look for unnecessary data, prompts, messages and unused screens. Eliminate unnecessary redundancies.

User control

User control means providing options for users to have some control over the system. Does the system control the options and pace, or does the user have control of some options? An example of offering user control is offering an advanced search as well as a simple search.

Match with user tasks

Matching with user tasks refers to how well the system matches the objectives found in the needs analysis and how well it reflects the tasks that users want to complete. Can users complete tasks as they expect and if users perceive the system as useful?

Note

1. For a description of the coined term 'satisficing', see Simon (1957).

Getting started

For university and college libraries, website and interface development can be a steady stream of projects ranging from full-scale library website interface designs or redesigns to smaller digital collection website interface development. Regardless of the size of the project, you need to do some preliminary planning. Before beginning any development project, you need to decide who will be involved in the design or redesign effort, what the project objectives are, what evaluation methods will be used, and how to recruit participants. This section describes the basics of preliminary planning and development. It includes assembling the development team, defining the project requirements, developing an evaluation plan, choosing an evaluation method and recruiting participants.

Preliminary steps

Assembling the development team

A crucial element in the early stages of website and interface design and development is determining who will participate as a member of the development team. Development teams today are multidisciplinary and represent many different specialists. They include specialists from content fields, design, development, human factors, multimedia and target user groups (Rubin 1994: 13). The development team will play a part in every stage of the development cycle from planning and designing through usability evaluation and testing. This team will work throughout the development cycle, providing their individual perspectives.

The use of a diverse team of people as members of the development team provides a rich source of information that feeds the design and development of the end-user interface. In his book *User Interface Evaluation*, Siegfried Treu (1994: 33) asserts that people are a source of information that informs the design and development of an interface. He describes the following groups:

- *Target users*, representatives of the population of people who will be using the website.

- *Surrogate users*, who take on the roles of target users and attempt to carry out the tasks target users might attempt.

- *User associates*, e.g. managers or colleagues, who provide information about goals, tasks and expectations.

- *Designers*, who provide information about design principles, factors, features, criteria, rationales, etc.

- (Experimental) *observers*, who are 'qualified to obtain evidence through direct observations' relative to human–computer interaction (HCI) performance, that is, how people interact with computers and computer systems; for example, the target website and the user interface.

- *Analysts and evaluators*, who have knowledge about evaluation, experimental design, and the analysis and interpretation of evaluative data. This group includes human factors researchers.

- *HCI experts*, who have knowledge of human–computer interaction, evaluation design and how to conduct formal tests and experiments. They can serve as specialists on the evaluation team. This group includes usability specialists.
- *Developers and implementers*, who have technical knowledge about tools and techniques related to interface design and software development.

The membership of the development team varies depending on the project scope, the project budget, the project requirements and the available personnel. For smaller, in-house projects, the development team might include the available personnel who represent the various groups mentioned above. If usability specialists or human factors researchers are not on staff, the team might consider hiring someone to complete the evaluations. However, even with a small budget, in-house staff can conduct usability evaluation methods to provide usability feedback. Rather than eliminating usability evaluation due to lack of specialists, it is better to have some feedback rather than none.

Define the project requirements

Before beginning the design and development of the end-user interface, that is, the front-end of the website, the development team needs to meet and decide what features, functions and content will be included. This is usually referred to as the requirements for the website (Usability.gov, year unknown: a). The team decides what specific components will be available in the back-end of the website, that is, what databases and functionality will be included. In addition they need to define the website goals and objectives, determine who will be using the website, and decide on usability goals and the usability evaluation plan. Information about the requirements will be used to design the final user-centred interface.

The requirements document summarises the project requirements and includes a description of the website design, the development plan and the evaluation plan. This document summarises the scope of the website, a description of the end-users, the features and functions, and the goals and objectives of the website. The requirements document also includes the details of the evaluation plan and the usability goals. This document is typically developed and approved by the development team. After the requirements have been determined, the development team is ready to begin the design of the end-user interface. Users and all stakeholders can be involved from the early stages of design through to completion.

What are the objectives?

The development team needs to decide the website objectives. In a university or college library website, the objectives need to be consistent with the university or college mission. More specifically, the objectives need to describe what the website will accomplish or how the website will address specific needs. For example, an objective might be to enable users to search multiple resources with one query using federated search software. The objectives of the website influence the design of the user interface.

What is the scope of the website?

University and college libraries need to determine exactly what will be offered on the target website and how the website will function based on budget, time and resource considerations. For example, if the website is an entire library website, then developers need to determine the extent of the information that will be offered, how it will be structured and categorised, and what functionality will be offered. If the target website is a special collection, the developers need to define the type of file formats, the size of the collection, the number of items, the amount of storage required, and how the collection will be searched, accessed and displayed.

The development team needs to determine how the information will be accessed and how the searches will function. In general, the team needs to know the details of the features and functions in order to plan an interface that will enable users to access the behind-the-scenes offerings.

Who are the end-users and what are their characteristics?

Defining the target user population is important to the design of the end-user interface. Novice users and expert users will interact with the interface differently. Likewise, those with and without background knowledge about the content will interact with the interface differently. University and college libraries need to decide who will be using the website so that the differences can be accommodated in the design.

If the website interface will be accessed primarily by the school's community, for example, then the audience is largely the students, faculty, staff and researchers. If the website is providing information on a worldwide basis, for example, a special digital collection, then the audience is the school's community, outside researchers and anyone with internet access. Once the team determines the primary user groups, they will need to describe user characteristics such as age, gender, expertise, domain knowledge, accessibility and any other characteristic that will affect website use.

What is the evaluation plan?

With the direction or guidance of a usability expert or human factors researcher, the team needs to develop an evaluation plan. The plan describes the usability evaluation methods and usability testing that will satisfy the usability goals of the product or website. As described by Lindgaard (1994: 249–81) and Rubin (1994: 83–9), the goal of an evaluation plan is to ensure that usability evaluation methods are part of the development process and, when feasible, the evaluation plan should include the items detailed below.

Usability goal statements

Usability goal statements describe the criteria for determining the usability of the website interface, that is, what the team strives to attain. Usability goals can be stated with general terms as well as specific quantitative terms. Goals are important because they help to focus the design and development of the website, and they describe acceptance criteria for the evaluation (Mayhew, 1999: 123–4).

Problem statements

A problem statement describes 'the issues and questions that need to be resolved and focuses the research' and activities associated with conducting the test (Rubin, 1994: 85). The statement needs to be clear and measurable to facilitate conducting a test that answers your questions and focuses the study.

Evaluation methods or test design

The evaluation methods or test design describe how you will carry out your research and the evaluation methods you will use. A usability specialist is often responsible for the test design because of their highly specialised skills.

User and task profiles

User and task profiles describe target user characteristics relative to the use of the website or product and a description of the tasks that are critical, typical, and those that are used frequently (see Chapter 3). Tasks can be described in terms of their level and impact:

- *Level of tasks*: This describes tasks that are typical for users to perform and the criticality of the task as it relates to danger and risk. For example, when software is used in medical circumstances or traffic control, errors can result in danger or risk to others.

- *Impact of the tasks*: Consider what tasks might pose problems for target users and the scale of the problems. The impact of the tasks is measured by the frequency that the problem occurs during typical use of the product and the severity of the problem, that is, the scale of the usability problem. The severity is described in terms of the impact on the user's ability to complete the task and recover from errors, and the likelihood that the user will encounter the error again. Because it is not likely that all problems can be addressed, the severity level will help the team to prioritise the problems.

What are the evaluation methods?

Some methods are better suited than others to generate information that will inform the design or redesign of the user interface, depending on the stage of development and the kind of information you need to generate. The usability evaluation methods described below and discussed in more detail later in this book are frequently used in usability evaluation (Lindgaard, 1994: 90–100, 113–32, 149–69; Jordan, 1998: 55–80; Torres, 2002: 225–8).

Questionnaires

Questionnaires are a means of collecting data, typically quantitative, from target users by posing questions to them. They can be administered online, in an e-mail or on paper. Comprised of structured items like multiple choice, rating scales or open-ended items, questionnaires are designed to collect information from potential users about such things as demographics, website use and website evaluation. They can be used in the early stages of development for needs analysis or in the late stages for evaluation.

Interviews

Interviews are used to elicit feedback about a broad or specific topic from participants. The researcher poses a series of questions surrounding an issue to participants to learn more about an issue. The questions can be loosely or highly structured depending on what you know and what you need to know. Interviews are useful at any stage of development, although contextual interviews are most effective in the early stages.

Person-to-person interview

In a person-to-person interview, questions are posed directly to the participant. Although they can be conducted by telephone, person-to-person interviews in usability evaluation usually take place in a face-to-face meeting of the researcher and the participant.

Contextual interviews

Contextual interviews are similar to think aloud protocols. The evaluator observes participants and records their discussions as they complete tasks using the target user interface. Unlike think aloud protocols, contextual interviews take place at the participant's typical workplace. This technique is most effective in the early stages of design, especially in a redesign effort, to learn more about issues related to the target website.

Focus groups

The focus group, sometimes referred to as a group interview, is a moderated discussion with a group of representative users or stakeholders who discuss a particular issue related to the library website design or redesign effort. They are used to identify preliminary concepts and ideas from representative users and also to learn more about users' characteristics. They are most effective in the early stages of development.

Participatory design

Participatory design describes methods that bring together stakeholders, most importantly representative users, to work towards developing a user-centred design. It embodies various methods which are most effective when used in the early stages of the design and development cycle. Methods include:

- *Affinity diagramming*: Used as a method of participatory design, this method involves all stakeholders and/or target users in the design of the website. The technique is especially useful for gathering direct feedback on how information is grouped. Participants write issues related to a specific topic on separate sticky notes (i.e. one issue per note). The notes are grouped by similarities. This method can also be used to group previously collected data. It is most useful in the early stages of development.

- *Card sorting*: This method is useful in grouping or categorising items listed on an end-user interface. Participants are presented with a group of cards labelled with link names, documents or other items from a website and are asked to group them into similar categories. The categories are discussed until reaching a decision while the conversation surrounding the activity is recorded. This activity is most useful in the early stages of development or in redesign efforts.

Prototyping

Prototyping is a method of evaluating the design of a website during the development of the website interface. An early paper prototype, a draft of the target website, can be as simple as a paper and pencil sketch. It is presented to target users and stakeholders for feedback about the usefulness and usability of the design. Paper prototyping is most useful in the early stages of development.

More sophisticated prototypes can be created during later stages of the development cycle. These can be computer-based designs and can be non-functional or functional prototypes. They can be used during usability testing of the website to gather feedback from target users.

Heuristic evaluation

Heuristic evaluation is a method of evaluating the website's usability by measuring it against a set of usability heuristics – widely accepted standards of user-centred design. Heuristic evaluation is most effective when conducted by multiple evaluators – specialists in the website domain and usability standards, who use common heuristics and procedures. This method is most effective when a prototype has been developed, although it can be used at any stage of development.

Cognitive walkthrough

Cognitive walkthrough is a method for evaluators to try out a set of realistic, typical tasks using a fairly detailed prototype, either paper or online, of the target website. Although this method can be used at any stage of development, it is often used in the early stages as a method of detecting early issues or problems.

Think aloud protocol

The think aloud protocol is a method of testing the completed website interface with representative target users. Participants are asked to complete a set of tasks using the target website interface or a working prototype of the website and to verbalise their thoughts while completing the tasks. A facilitator observes and records the session to detect issues or problems with the website and creates a report summarising the findings and found issues. The findings feed the redesign of the website as part of an iterative design process. This method is most effective when the development of website interface or a working prototype is complete. This is usually in the later stages of development.

Recruiting participants

After selecting the evaluation method and making some preliminary plans for the evaluation (e.g. dates, length of time and incentives), the development team will need to determine who will be included as participants in the evaluation study. This will vary depending on the evaluation method used. Some evaluation methods, such as heuristic evaluation or expert reviews, include only the evaluators who review the user interface for usability defects. However, most other evaluation methods will include participants who represent the targeted population of users or other stakeholders.

Although participants usually include target users, they can vary depending on the type of evaluation. For example, participants in a participatory design group can include representative stakeholders from content experts to end-users as well as target users. If you are completing think aloud protocols, participants are representatives of the target population of end-users. In the sections of this book that describe in more detail the specifics of the evaluation methods (surveys, questionnaires, interviews, participatory design, prototyping, heuristic evaluation, cognitive walkthrough, and think aloud protocols) you will find more about the participants recommended for each method.

Many evaluation methods involve participants from the target population. The target population includes the people who typically access the website. Because the group of target users is usually too large to select everyone, we select a smaller group that shares the specific characteristics of the target users; this is referred to as a representative sample.

Select a representative group of participants

When selecting target users as participants in usability evaluation, it is important to select a representative group in order to detect problems that are associated with different user groups. For example, a website that might be easy for an experienced user might be very difficult for a novice user. Jordan (1998) suggests considering the following characteristics when selecting participants in usability evaluation.

Experience

The experience that people have had with the website or software or similar products can affect how they complete tasks. People who have previously used the website or software will most likely find the tasks easier to complete than those who are using the website for the first time. You can expect that those with experience, who are familiar with the options, menus and conventions in the design, will take less time to learn the new system and will experience fewer problems. Novice or first-time users will take longer to learn the website and will experience more problems.

Experience with other similar products

Experience with other similar products can also affect how people operate the target website. For example, if you are evaluating a new federated search product, participants who are familiar with other federated search products will most likely draw on previous experience to learn the target website.

This type of experience can also be detrimental if the new product is completely different from the previous website and contrary to the user's expectations. For example, consider an experienced user of a standard keyboard trying out a completely new keyboard layout.

Domain knowledge

Domain knowledge refers to the person's knowledge about the field of study. In the case of a university or college library website, knowledge about the types of resources available or methods of creating an effective search query can be an advantage in learning a new website or software.

Cultural background

Cultural background can affect a person's use of a new website or software interface. People from countries other than the USA might be familiar with different methods of categorisation or groupings of resources, other libraries, cultural behaviour or different languages. Language barriers can affect a person's ability to understand written language terminology used on websites or their ability to design an effective search query.

Disability

Website interfaces that are easy for able-bodied people to use might be difficult to use for those with disabilities. For example, people who are visually-impaired and colour-blind might not be able to read some text due to limited contrast of colours; those who are hearing-impaired might not be able to hear audio and will need written text as an alternative; and users with physical disabilities such as arthritis or those with limited movement might have problems with mouse movements. These problems can be detected by being aware of standards of design for accessibility and also by including representative users, including the disabled, in the evaluation.

Age and gender

Age and gender can be factors to consider when assessing the usability of website interfaces. Younger users, who have grown up with technology, might have an easier time learning to use a website than older users with less experience with technology. Gender also might be a factor. Females might be more concerned with the aesthetics of the website, and males might prefer a more 'high-tech' product.

Consider recruiting issues

Although recruiting representative participants for evaluation activities is useful to detect problems associated with diverse user groups, the process can be time-consuming. The entire procedure of scheduling one participant might take up to two hours (Barnum, 2002: 189). Recruiting involves sending out a request, screening the volunteers to determine who will provide a representative sample, scheduling, and various other communicating e-mails or letters.

For college and university libraries, the target population for library websites is often the members of the school's community. Although some digital collections target outside the community, the primary population is the students, faculty, staff or other members of the school's community. The sample could include diverse affiliations (students, faculty and staff), disciplines, level of computer expertise, first language, and any other characteristic you feel would represent the population of users. You can check with the placement office and ask for a sample of students, staff and faculty to serve as the recruitment sample.

You can use incentives to encourage a better response to recruitment efforts. While contributing to the development of the design of a library website user interface is a basic incentive, offering something tangible can encourage participation. We generally offer a monetary incentive of $20 to entice participation, although other incentives such as food (e.g. focus group lunch) or credit for food providers or book stores can work as well.

Recruiting large samples of participants

Some evaluation methods, such as needs assessment questionnaires, involve large groups of participants. The participants are selected from the target population. It is unlikely you will be able to involve the entire population in your study, so it is necessary to select a smaller group; this is referred to as the sample. As with all evaluation methods, you need to select a representative group of participants for the sample. This means that the sample will be similar to the population with respect to individual characteristics.

One method of recruiting a representative sample is to select a random sample of the population. A random sample entails selecting participants in a manner whereby every user has an opportunity to be selected (similar to a lottery draw). Larger random samples are generally considered to have similar attributes to the population.

To determine the size of the sample, you first need to determine how many participants you need. CustomInsight.com (year unknown) offers some suggestions on selecting a random sample, determining sample size, error and confidence levels. They suggest that not everyone who receives the recruitment letter (i.e. the invitation to participate in the evaluation) will take the survey. You need to determine how many people to recruit to have an acceptable number of responses. Generally when using a cold call for participants you can consider about a 25 per cent response rate. This means that if you want 100 people to respond, you need to send the recruitment letter to a random sample of 400. If you expect a higher response rate, for example 50 per cent, you would send the recruitment letter to a random sample of 200.

If you want to be certain that you have represented the user groups, you might consider using a stratified random sample. This means randomly sampling each user group, for example, students, faculty and staff. If the groups are different sizes, you can follow the same procedure as in a random sample of the population, although with each group.

In both methods of recruiting, people choose whether to respond; in other words, they self-select. Self-selection can result in participants whose motivation is spurred by problems or issues they have with your website. Although you might be interested in their feedback, remember that they might not represent the views of the general population (Brinck, Gergle and Wood, 2002: 80). If you are interested in finding problems with your website, self-selection might yield participants who can be especially helpful.

Recruiting small samples of participants

Most usability evaluation methods (e.g. think aloud protocols, card sorting, prototyping) will use a small group of representative users. You need to determine what method to use to recruit volunteers and how to screen them in order to select a representative sample.

When recruiting, check the likely places to find participants and the information sources they frequently check. For libraries, these often include physical or intranet bulletin boards, library student workers, and referrals from librarians or faculty. Other places to recruit are newspaper advertisements, college or university placement offices and qualified friends (Barnum, 2002: 191–2). A common method of recruiting volunteers is to post a recruitment letter on an intranet or physical bulletin board and ask volunteers to reply. Some libraries have a pool of volunteers who have responded to an earlier request to become future participants in usability evaluation methods. You can also recruit by posting a message on your website.

Electronic methods of recruiting offer the advantage of including an embedded link to a screening survey. Alternatively, screening questionnaires can be e-mailed, mailed or faxed to volunteers. Regardless of the method that is used, a screening questionnaire is used to collect specific information from volunteers that will inform your selection decisions.

Using a screening questionnaire

The screening questionnaire is used to select a representative sample. You can screen using an interview conducted on the phone or face-to-face, in an e-mail, with a computer-based questionnaire, or with a paper questionnaire (Rubin, 1994:

142–4). Important information to include in a screening questionnaire is the volunteer's name, contact information (home or work phone, e-mail) age or year in school, discipline, first language and gender. Other common information includes the type of computer and browser, and experience with computers and types of software.

Add any additional information that is specific to your objectives and to the design of the website. For example, when developing a website interface that includes search engine software, it is important to screen for experience with search software. An example of a question to determine experience with search software is shown in Figure 2.1.

The introduction page of the screening questionnaire can be used to provide information about the evaluation, the screening questionnaire, and the research team. Use this page to inform volunteers about why you are contacting them. Explain why you are using the questionnaire and about how long it will take to complete it. Let volunteers know that their answers will be confidential and used only by the research group.

Before using the questionnaire with potential participants, conduct a pilot test with colleagues or students working in the library. This will help you to determine if your questions are clear, and if you are getting the answers that will help you to select participants. After all volunteers

| Figure 2.1 | Example of a question to determine experience with search software |

Please check all of the following search engines that you have used.

☐ Google   ☐ Yahoo   ☐ Library catalogues

☐ Federated searches ☐ Library databases   ☐ Other

have completed the questionnaire, you are ready to select participants.

Using the responses on the screening questionnaire, you can select a sample with the characteristics of the general population. Although the sample size will be too small to generalise to the population, it will still provide an idea of how different user groups (e.g. novices versus experienced users) will interact with the interface.

After selecting a representative sample, notify all the volunteers about the results, the details of the session, scheduling and their compensation. Remind participants of the time and location of the session a day or two before the session. Despite all of your efforts, you can still expect some no-shows. You might try to schedule one or two extra participants, in case of this.

What is informed consent?

During any evaluation procedure, the participants' rights, interests and dignity need to be protected. Participants who are involved in the usability evaluation must be fully informed of the procedures, risks, and their rights and confidentiality issues related to participation in the usability evaluation. Confidentiality is ensuring that the information generated in usability studies and reported in papers and/or presentations cannot be linked to individual participants. Confidentiality guarantees that the privacy of individuals will be protected and identifying information will not be released to individuals who are not directly involved in the study.

This information needs to be summarised in a written document for participants to read and then give their written consent to participate, usually by signing the document. This is referred to as informed consent. Although it is helpful to discuss the nature and details of the study session, a consent form should be used to gain written consent from participants. Dumas and Redish (1999: 204–8) suggest including the following in a consent form:

- *Information*: Explain the procedures, the purpose of the session, the risks to the participant, the opportunity to ask questions, and the opportunity to withdraw at any time without penalty.

- *Comprehension*: Convey the information clearly and completely, neither rushing through the procedures nor making them seem unimportant.

- *Voluntariness*: The participants need to be aware that participation is voluntary and without undue influence from the organisers of the testing. You need to remain neutral when participants consider withdrawing.

- *Participants' rights*: The participants need to know that they can withdraw at any time, can ask for a break, will have their privacy and confidentiality protected, and know what the test is about and how the results will be used.

A sample consent form is included in the appendix.

3

User needs analysis

In addition to creating a website interface that is user-centred and easy to use, developers need to create a website that is useful and meets the expectations of the target users; this is all the more difficult because people do not always know what they want. This stage can be accomplished by completing a user needs analysis. This is an important stage – the website and interface design will be based on this information. Faulty assumptions or goals will lead to a faulty design that is difficult to fix once in place. It is easier and less expensive to design a user-centred system from the beginning than it is to fix a completed and in-service system that is difficult to use and fails to meet user needs and expectations.

The objective of a user needs analysis is to: (a) identify the end-users' goals for the website, (b) define the end-users' characteristics and expectations, (c) determine what functionality will be included, (d) set usability objectives, and (e) determine how the website will operate (Lindgaard, 1994: 38–49; Brinck, Gergle and Wood, 2002: 64–72). In addition, this is a good time to complete a task analysis, that is, to determine what tasks meet users' needs and expectations. For a redesign, in addition to the previously listed objectives, this stage will be used to determine the problems associated with the interface that is currently in place.

Based on the number of computer systems that are either little used or not used at all, developers often do not know or understand users' needs. Often communication between developers and target users is hampered by misunderstandings because both groups tend to speak different languages; they are influenced by different backgrounds, perceptions and beliefs; and developers often fail to understand that they are different from typical users (Lindgaard, 1994: 38–49; Brinck et al., 2002: 64–72). The objectives of needs analysis include the following (Lindgaard, 1994: 38–49; Brinck et al., 2002: 64–72):

- *Define the audience*: Determine who will be the primary users of the website. Determine users' characteristics (e.g. gender and age), accessibility needs, and computer and software experience.

- *Identify user goals*: Determine what users expect, want and need from the system. Examine how they solve their problems now, and what they would like to do with a new system. Determine what tasks they expect and desire to perform using the system.

- *Set usability objectives*: Determine to what extent the website needs to satisfy both users' and the organisation's usability goals and how to measure success. In this stage, identify how frequently the website will be used, the length of the average visit, and how many errors people will tolerate before abandoning their tasks.

- *Identify the design constraints*: Define the budget, the time line, and the project team. Investigate target platforms and their technical limitations and possible constraints that will apply.

- *Define functional specifications*: Based on all of your goals, design constraints and the task analysis, specify the detailed functionality of the website. For example, consider what tasks people will complete with the website, what pages to include, whether to include contact information and a help section, and decide on a method of responding to errors.

Several methods can be used to inform a user needs analysis. One method of determining needs is a task analysis – an analysis of the tasks and a detailed description of the method of completing a task. Another method of collecting data to define users and to determine their needs and expectations is a survey – either a questionnaire or an interview. These methods are described in the following sections.

Task analysis

A task analysis is the process of determining the goals and objectives of the website, the primary tasks that will enable people to accomplish their goals, and a detailed description of the steps needed to complete tasks (Hackos and Redish, 1998: 11–13). A task is what the people need to do to achieve their desired results. For example, a task might be to find books using the online library catalogue.

A task analysis describes what actions people need to take and/or the cognitive processes (mental thoughts and activities) that are necessary in order to complete the tasks. The analysis describes the step-by-step process people take to complete tasks. The results of a task analysis will provide the means of prioritising tasks and the basis for designing a useful system. A task analysis is also used for developing scenarios for evaluation methods such as think aloud protocols and cognitive walkthroughs.

Before beginning the task analysis, you need to decide what tasks people are interested in completing using the system. 'The most crucial component of task analysis is gaining a deep understanding of the goals people are trying to achieve' (Brinck et al., 2002: 96). The description of the major goals of the target website and people's reasons for accessing the website provide the basis for the specific task. For each specific goal, describe a task and complete a task analysis. Booth describes a task analysis by saying:

> A task analysis, in the usability sense of the term, involves listing the user's goals. In this list the overall goal is usually the end-result the user might wish to achieve using the proposed system, while the user's sub-goals can provide a perspective on the tasks that need to be performed to achieve the overall goal. Furthermore, these sub-goals provide some idea of the order in which tasks need to be performed. (Booth, 1999: 114)

For example, a typical goal for a library website would be to complete a search for information resources using the library catalogue. For this example, you need to determine what actions the user will take to complete the search and what the user needs to know in order to complete the search. The description of the necessary actions and the mental process is the task analysis.

What is the objective?

The objective of a task analysis is to understand the user's reasons for accessing the website, what they need to do to achieve their goals, and how their previous knowledge affects the actions they take to complete a task and achieve their goals (Hackos and Redish, 1998: 7–8). A task analysis is the basis for designing a user-centred website and the basis for creating scenarios and tasks that are used in think aloud protocols, cognitive walkthroughs and other evaluation methods.

How long will it take?

The amount of time needed to complete a task analysis is dependent on the method that you use to collect information. After the information has been collected, compiled and summarised, the actual task analysis, the description of the primary tasks and a breakdown of the actions and mental processes needed to complete each task, will take a few days to a week.

How do you complete a task analysis?

You can gain information about users' goals and objectives for the proposed website and what tasks they want to accomplish by surveying representative users (see the section on surveys, questionnaires and interviews). Interviews include person-to-person interviews, contextual interviews and group interviews (focus groups). Surveys, including both questionnaires and interviews, are discussed in the following section.

You can complete a contextual interview and observe representative users in their working environment as they complete tasks using the target website or an existing website (see the section on contextual inquiry). Site visits will yield information about what tasks are important to users, how users complete tasks and what problems they have, as well as enable you to learn about the influences of their environment on task completion.

After you have collected the data to determine website objectives and have defined and prioritised users' tasks, you can analyse each primary task with respect to the actions and mental processes that are needed to complete it. An approach to task analysis includes the following stages (Hackos and Redish, 1998: 7–8):

- Identify and prioritise the overall tasks and the characteristics of the environment in which people will work. Prioritise the tasks based on the frequency of use and their importance. Describe tasks in terms of the objectives for the website.

- Select the primary and most frequently used tasks and identify the subtasks for each of the broad task definitions. You might find four to eight subtasks for each. For smaller websites you might choose all of the broad tasks for this stage; for larger websites, choose the primary tasks.

- For each subtask, identify the steps or actions and mental processes needed to complete the subtask.

- Determine the most efficient way to complete the task and whether it is based on logic or affected by previous knowledge and/or experience.

What are the advantages?

A task analysis is an opportunity to discover and prioritise the tasks people expect to complete with your website. Based on this information, it is an opportunity to define the scope of your website and to analyse task completion from the end-user's point of view, enabling designers and developers to focus on the user's goals and objectives. The task analysis enables designers to determine ways to make task completion more efficient and user-centred.

What are the disadvantages?

Onsite observations of users can take longer to schedule and complete than other methods of evaluation, and compilation and analysis of the data can be time-consuming. If the task analysis is used as a basis for design recommendations, designers might favour efficiency of task completion (decreasing the number of actions required to complete tasks) over effort required for task completion. Task analysis is therefore not an effective method of determining the degree of difficulty of the task (Jordan, 1998: 75).

Surveys

A survey is a method of collecting information by posing a series of questions to representative members of the targeted population. 'A survey may serve a single or several purposes, and it is simply a method for systematically collecting information on a given topic or topics from a number of people' (Lindgaard, 1994: 161). The two basic categories of surveys are questionnaires and interviews, although each method has variations within the group (Trochim, 2000).

Questionnaires, often paper and pencil, can also be administered as a computer-based or online questionnaire. The questionnaire can be comprised of one-word or short-answer items, open-ended or essay-type items, and rating-scale items that measure attitudes and feelings (e.g. Likert scale). They are usually designed based on some prior knowledge of the relevant issues.

Interviews can be administered person-to-person as a face-to-face interview in which the researcher poses questions directly to the participant or as a telephone interview. They can also be administered in a field setting in which the interviewer visits participants in their place of work to conduct a face-to-face interview.

Interviews can be structured, similar to questionnaires, semi-structured, and unstructured using general open-ended items. Semi-structured interviews are generally designed when the researcher wants to explore the issues. Group interviews, usually referred to as focus groups, are a group discussion around an issue which is guided by a moderator.

What is the objective?

The objective of the survey depends on the method that is used and the stage in the development cycle during which it is administered. Early in the development cycle, surveys can be used to determine user needs, preferences, characteristics and expectations for the functionality and design of the target website and the end-user interface.

In the mid-stages of the website development cycle, surveys can be used to provide feedback about the issues related to an early website design. The feedback can be used to refine the website or system design with respect to the user interface design or the functionality of the website. In the final stages of the cycle, surveys can be used to evaluate the final design of the website and the end-user interface and to refine the design towards creating a user-centred interface. Surveys can be used to collect the following data (Brinck et al., 2002: 72–4):

- *Demographics*: Surveys can be used to collect data about target users' characteristics, e.g. age, gender, job or major area of study, education level, level of computer expertise, and first language. You can also learn about target users' experience and knowledge as it relates to the proposed website.

- *Needs and preferences*: Surveys can be used to identify problems people have with current products or those similar to the proposed product, what features they expect the product to include, and how they expect to use the product.

- *Design impact*: Design impact includes questions that will yield information that is relevant to the design of the website and the end-user interface. Let participants know that the information will be used to inform the design of the product.

Who are the participants?

Participants, although usually representatives of the target population, can also be any stakeholder or member of the development team. This includes the designers, developers, managers and administrators. Determining who to include in your survey largely depends on the objectives of the survey.

Early in the development cycle you might survey representative users, content experts and the development group for feedback regarding the scope of the content, the important issues and limitations. Late in the development cycle, surveys can be used to evaluate a completed website. As in other evaluation methods, surveying target users or other stakeholders provides the perspectives on website and end-user interface design that are useful at any stage of the development.

What are the advantages?

Surveys are methods of obtaining information that feeds the design of a user-centred website. They can be used at any stage of the development cycle.

What are the disadvantages?

In general, a disadvantage of surveys is that they do not provide data about the direct interaction of users with the website. 'One cannot always take user statements at face value. Data about people's actual behavior should have precedence over people's claims of what they *think* they do' (Nielsen, 1993: 209). In addition, designing surveys requires some expertise. More specific advantages and disadvantages vary depending on the chosen method and are discussed in the following sections.

Questionnaires

Surveying people using questionnaires is appropriate during any stage of the development cycle and can be used with both large and small sample groups. Implementation and distribution vary depending on the objectives of the questionnaire and the point in the development cycle when they are used. They vary in length from a long needs assessment questionnaire conducted early in the cycle to a short ten-point scale administered as a post-test evaluation after a think aloud protocol. This section describes the different types of questionnaires and the advantages and disadvantages of each type.

What is a questionnaire?

A questionnaire is a method of surveying participants by asking them to answer questions, complete a rating scale, or respond to statements about a relevant issue. 'The questionnaire, designed to ask a series of structured and uniform questions, is essentially a written interview which can easily be administered to a large number of people' (Lindgaard, 1994: 161). Questionnaires appear to be an easy method of surveying a large group of people, although in order to collect reliable and valid data, a great deal of planning and expertise is needed to develop a useful questionnaire. Participants are more likely to complete a questionnaire that is easy to understand and quick to complete, however, it should also be long enough to yield valid information (Lindgaard, 1994: 165).

Questionnaires are often implemented using paper and pencil methods and distributed through the mail, to groups, or directly person-to-person. More recently, questionnaires have been administered online or made available electronically. The link to an online questionnaire can be provided in a similar manner as paper and pencil methods, that is, through postal mail, to groups, or directly person-to-person.

The questionnaire can be comprised of one-word or short-answer items, multiple-choice items, open-ended or essay-type items, and scale items (e.g. Likert scale) that measure attitudes and feelings. They are usually designed based on some prior knowledge of the relevant issues. The length of a questionnaire varies depending on the objective. As described below, questionnaires can be used in a mail survey, e-mail survey, electronic survey, group administered or individually administered survey, or drop-off survey (Lindgaard, 1994: 167; Trochim, 2000; Barribeau et al., 2005).

Mail survey

The questionnaire is mailed to the sample of target users. To encourage participation, include a self-addressed, stamped envelope for returning the completed questionnaire, and alert possible respondents in advance of the questionnaire. A mail survey is useful if you want to randomly sample the university community during a needs assessment survey. Using this method you can also stratify the sample over the user groups.

Advantages: Mail surveys are less expensive to administer than drop-off, group or individually administered surveys. Participants can complete the surveys at their convenience. There is little chance for administrator bias, such as is possible with person-to-person or group surveys. It is possible to define a sample group and to distribute to a large sample group.

Disadvantages: The greatest disadvantage of mail surveys is the lower response rate compared with other types of survey. The response rate is often about 25 per cent with a mail survey. Lacking the personal presence of an administrator, questions about the survey cannot be answered.

E-mail survey

The e-mail survey is similar to a regular mail survey, only distributed by e-mail. The questionnaire can be attached to the e-mail and downloaded and returned to the sender either in the postal mail or in an e-mail. An alternative is to include an embedded link to an electronic survey.

Advantages: The advantages are similar to the mail survey, although e-mail surveys are even less expensive to administer. Participants can complete the surveys at their convenience. There is little chance for administrator bias. It is possible to define a sample group and to distribute to a large sample group.

Disadvantages: Like the mail survey, the greatest disadvantage is the lower response rate for e-mail surveys compared with other types of survey. Lacking the personal presence of an administrator, questions about the survey cannot be answered, although, with an e-mail survey, participants can e-mail the sender with questions.

Group or individually administered survey

Group administered surveys are distributed to a group of people, such as a focus group, which is meeting to discuss an issue. People can complete a questionnaire following the discussion. Individually administered surveys are distributed personally to the participants. For example, participants might complete a questionnaire following a think aloud protocol session.

Advantages: Group or individually administered surveys have a much better response rate than other types of surveys, and you get the survey results quickly. Participants have an opportunity to ask questions to clarify the meaning of the questions.

Disadvantages: This method is best when used with a small, specific sample, for example, the development team or a focus group. Scheduling can be a problem unless the survey is used with other scheduled evaluation sessions.

Drop-off survey

This type of survey is hand-delivered to the participants. For example, if you are redesigning the library website and would like input from library users, you might pass the questionnaires to everyone who enters the library on a given day(s). Surveys can be returned in a drop-off box, collected by the interviewer, or returned in the mail.

Advantages: When the survey is distributed personally, the response rate is usually higher than a mail or e-mail survey. Participants can complete the survey privately and at their convenience and ask questions of the facilitator.

Disadvantages: This type of survey takes considerably longer for the facilitator to administer than a mail or e-mail survey. Because of the personal contact, you have less control of the sample and cannot guarantee a random or representative sample.

Electronic survey

The electronic or web-based questionnaire, like the paper and pencil questionnaire, is a structured sequence of questions, but it is a computer-based, electronic survey. The electronic survey is constructed using software specifically designed for web-based survey development.

Electronic surveys can be made available to the participants in several ways. They can be part of an e-mail which can be completed electronically and returned to the sender by e-mail. The surveys can be available on computers that are publicly-available, for example, in libraries. The link to a web-based survey can be embedded in an e-mail that is sent to the sample group, or it can be posted as a link on a website.

Advantages: Web-based surveys are convenient and easy for participants to complete. They are less expensive and take less time to administer. Response rates are often higher than paper-based mail and e-mail surveys and often have a quicker response time. As well saving a great deal of time for the administrators, some web-based survey data collection systems also include data analysis.

Disadvantages: With web-based surveys, you might have difficulty ensuring confidentiality. The sample group is limited to those who have a computer, and, as with many computer-based activities, it is possible to have technical problems with the software. Designers of web-based surveys need to have some knowledge of the application software used with the survey.

What is the length and objective of a questionnaire?

Questionnaires can be used to evaluate the design or the end-user interface and the functionality of a website or survey attitudes and perceptions. A screening questionnaire is used to collect data that informs the selection of representative users in usability evaluation activities.

The length of a questionnaire can also vary. It can be as short as a ten-item attitude scale that takes a few minutes to complete. Short questionnaires can be used following a think aloud protocol session to screen volunteers for participation in an evaluation. A lengthy needs assessment questionnaire might take about 20 to 30 minutes to complete.

The challenge is to design a questionnaire that is long enough to be useful and short enough to encourage participation (Barnum, 2002: 47). As shown in Table 3.1,

Table 3.1   Suggestions for survey length

Survey type	No. questions
Individual survey	20
Group survey	100
Mail	60
Phone	20

Source: Lindgaard (1994: 163).

Lindgaard (1994) suggests that the length of the questionnaire should vary depending on the type of survey.

Who are the participants?

The participants can be recruited from stakeholder groups including content experts, designers and developers, and members of the population. Determining who to select for the sample group depends on the objective of the questionnaire and the stage in the development cycle.

During the early stages of design, representatives from all stakeholder groups, content experts, designers and developers, and target users can yield information about the development issues, and usability issues. Participants in the evaluation of the website are usually target users.

How long will it take?

To complete an evaluation using a questionnaire could take from a couple of days to several weeks depending on the length and type of questionnaire and how you report the findings. You need time for development, recruiting, pilot testing, implementation, analysing the data and writing the report. A shorter screening or post-test questionnaire would probably take less than a week. A longer needs assessment questionnaire would probably take several weeks.

The length of time for participants to complete a questionnaire varies depending on the type and purpose. Determining the desired completion time in advance will affect the number and type of items in the questionnaire. A questionnaire for a needs assessment might take 20–30 minutes, while one that follows a think aloud protocol might take 5–10 minutes. Timing can be determined during pilot testing.

How do I design a questionnaire?

Identify the problem and define goals and objectives

Trochim (2000) maintains that three important considerations in questionnaire design are: (a) determining the question content, scope and purpose; (b) choosing the response format for collecting information from the respondent; and (c) figuring out how to word the question to get at the issue of interest.

To address these considerations, first decide the purpose of the questionnaire, that is, how the information will be used. When defining the purpose, you need to consider the goals and the objectives. The goals and objectives will influence the choice of participants, the design of questionnaire items, and the distribution methods.

Well-defined goals lead to a well-designed questionnaire. Poorly designed questionnaires are the most frequent reasons for poor results from a questionnaire (StatPac, year unknown; Trochim, 2000). Goals are simply one or two clear sentences that describe the purpose of the questionnaire. For example, a goal of a needs analysis questionnaire might be stated as, 'Determine the basic characteristics of the target user group'. Using this goal as a guide, items can be developed that generate information that responds to this goal. They might include the questions shown in Figure 3.1 (Mayhew, 1999: 49–55).

Figure 3.1	Sample questions to determine characteristics of user groups

---

1. What is your name? _____

2. Do you enjoy learning how to use new software applications?
_____ Yes, it's usually challenging and interesting.
_____ Sometimes, depending on the application.
_____ No, it's usually tedious and frustrating.
_____ Other (please explain) _____

Design the questionnaire items (questions and statements)

The design of your questionnaire and the format of the specific questions are influenced by the desire to keep the survey short, thereby enabling quick completion time, to provide results that are easily analysed using statistical tools, to encourage respondents to answer completely and honestly, and to yield results that address your research questions and generate new information (Brinck et al., 2002: 74–8).

Questionnaire item formats can include multiple choice, short answer, checklists, rank ordering questions, attitude scales (e.g. Likert response scales), and open-ended, essay-type items, as described below (Lindgaard, 1994: 170–2; Trochim, 2000; Brinck et al., 2002: 74–8; Barribeau et al., 2005).

Multiple choice

A multiple choice item includes several choices of answers or category of response to a statement or question enabling you to restrict respondents' answers. Multiple choice items are useful when you know that the responses will be limited to a known set of possibilities.

When possibilities are limited to a few of the most frequently used responses, although different responses are possible, include 'Other' as a choice. Multiple choice items can be analysed using statistical methods. They typically use radio buttons to limit selection to only one response.

Checklist

A variation of the multiple choice question is the checklist. In a checklist, participants are asked a question and given a list of statements or items from which they choose as many responses as are relevant to the question. Checklists are quick and easy for participants to complete. A checklist typically uses checkboxes to enable more than one response. See Figure 3.2 for an example of a checklist.

Short answer

In a short answer question, people respond to a question using a few words, as shown in Figure 3.3. Short answer questions are useful for collecting demographic information especially when surveying only a small sample. As respondents might use different formats for indicating the same response, you will need to summarise the survey results by hand. For example, students in the field of

Figure 3.2 Example of a checklist

Which of the following have you used? Check all that apply.

☐ library catalogue   ☐ multi-database search   ☐ CiteSeer

☐ library databases   ☐ Google   ☐ Yahoo

☐ Amazon   ☐ Other searches _____

Figure 3.3 Examples of short answer questions

What is your name? _____

What is your major field(s) of study? _____

computer science might respond to 'What is your major field(s) of study?' with CS, comp. sci., computer science, or SCS. If you are surveying a large sample, consider a checklist of standardised responses for easier analysis.

Rank order items

With rank order items, participants order the entire list of items or a subset of the list. Using numerals they indicate the 'most important' to the 'least important'. The list choices range from a statement to a one-word item. Rank ordering a subset of the list is easier for participants to complete and might also be easier for you to analyse. See Figure 3.4 for an example of a rank order question.

Rating scale

A rating scale is a method of quantifying subjective ratings of attitudes and opinions often using rating scales such as

Figure 3.4 Example of a rank ordering question

What do you use on the library's website? Indicate the three most important by labelling them 1 (first), 2 (second), and 3 (third).

☐ library catalogue   ☐ research help   ☐ interlibrary loan

☐ library databases   ☐ reserves   ☐ full text resources

☐ user account info   ☐ online journals   ☐ other _____

the Likert or the Thurstone scale. In usability evaluation, attitude measures are used to gauge users' attitudes and perceptions about the usability and design of the end-user's website or website interface. Using a Likert-type scale, participants choose from a five or seven point scale to indicate their degree of agreement with a statement.

Other types of attitude scales might include other choices, for example, 'extremely difficult' to 'extremely easy', 'very often' to 'almost never', or 'very clear' to 'very confusing'. Include an 'N/A' choice for questions that are not applicable to the respondent's own experience with the website. See Figure 3.5 for an example of rating scale items from a survey of library website users.

Open-ended essay-type items

In open-ended, essay-type items, the respondents need to write their answers. The answers are usually a few to several sentences and give participants an opportunity to express their opinions, suggestions and comments. Open-ended items yield a broad range of ideas and comments.

Although open-ended items yield a wide range of responses, the drawback is that analysing the results can be difficult and time-consuming. Be sure to leave plenty of

Figure 3.5   An example of rating scale items

Please rate the following by circling a rating from 1 to 5.
Circle NA when the item is not applicable or when you don't know.

I use the library website . . .	Frequency of Use					
For accessing library catalogues, databases, reference materials, full-text books, journals, newspapers, etc.	almost never 1	2	3	4	very often 5	NA 0
For general information about services: reference, borrowing, reserves, interlibrary loan, etc.	almost never 1	2	3	4	very often 5	NA 0

Figure 3.6	Examples of open-ended questions

What suggestions do you have for improving the website?

If you could change anything on the website, what would you change and how would you change it?

room for the responses. See Figure 3.6 for an example of an open-ended question.

Use clear wording for the questionnaire items

The wording of the item is critical to the success of the questionnaire. Poorly worded items can be misunderstood, leading to problematic results. For example, in a needs assessment survey, the examples in Figure 3.7 are used to determine frequency of use for computer, software or website elements. The two items ask the same question and offer the same choices, however, they are worded differently.

Item A lacks definition for the levels of use, therefore the degree of use is open to interpretation. Participants need to know what is meant by 'Low'. Some participants might think that 'three times' is low while others might think that 'five times' is low. Using additional definitions for each level as shown in Item B ensures that the results are clear and not open to interpretation by the participant.

The design of questions can affect the results. A clearly worded question using terminology that is understandable to respondents will usually produce results that are valid and reliable. In order to develop well-designed questions,

Figure 3.7	Sample questions that show vaguely defined choices and clearly defined choices

Question A: (not recommended) This example shows a question in which the choices for the degree of use are questionable and open to interpretation.

How would you describe how frequently you used the library online catalogue during the Spring semester 2007?

____ None

____ Low

____ Moderately low

____ Moderately high

____ High

Question B: (recommended) This example shows a question in which the choices for the degree of use are more defined.

How would you describe how frequently you used the library online catalogue during the Spring semester 2007?

____ None, I have never used the library online catalogue .

____ Low, I have used the library online catalogue 1 to 3 times

____ Moderately low, I have used the library online catalogue 4 to 6 times

____ Moderately high, I have used the library online catalogue 7 to 10 times

____ High, I have used the library online catalogue more than 10 times

____ Other (please describe) _____

consider the questions below (Trochim, 2000; Barribeau et al., 2005; IAR, 2007).

Can the question be misunderstood; is it ambiguous?

When designing items in a questionnaire, be as clear as possible and avoid vague, seldom used, or technical terminology. Do participants know what is meant by terminology that is frequently used in libraries, for example, 'federated search' or 'full-text'? Determine the appropriate use of terminology during pilot testing with representative users.

Figure 3.8 Example of questionnaire items that show problems with prerequisite knowledge

Item A: I will definitely use the new multi-resource search (federated search) product in the next month.

Item B: I will definitely use the new multi-resource search (federated search) product in the next month if I need to find resources.

What assumptions does the question make?

Consider what participants need to know in order to respond to the item and whether they have the requisite knowledge to respond accurately. For example, consider the statement in Item A shown in Figure 3.8. Do participants know what they will be doing in the next month or can the phrasing be changed to accommodate need, as in Item B?

Specify the timeframe

When questions refer to a timeframe, be sure that this is specified. When the timeframe is vague, as in Item A in Figure 3.9, respondents might interpret it differently. Some might interpret 'recently' as in the last week while others might think it is in the last month. A specifically defined timeframe, as in Item B, will result in more consistent interpretations and thus valid results.

Figure 3.9 Example of questionnaire items that show problems with vague timeframe

Item A – vague: Have you visited the library website recently?

Item B – better: Have you visited the library website in January 2008?

| Figure 3.10 | Example of questionnaire items showing personal versus less personal wording |

Item A: Less personal: The website is easy to use.

Item B: More personal: Are you satisfied that the website is easy to use?

How personal is the wording?

Items can be designed that are relatively impersonal to relatively personal. In the example shown in Figure 3.10, Item A is less personal than Item B. It is important that the level is appropriate to the context of the questionnaire and that you use that level consistently. If you decide you want personal wording, do it throughout the questionnaire.

Other wording issues

Other wording issues include:

- *Terminology*: Does the question contain difficult or unclear terminology? Consider that some terms require specialised knowledge to understand or may fall under the realm of library terminology.
- *Consistency*: Do you use wording consistently throughout the questionnaire or does it change even though you are referring to the same thing?
- *Single concept*: Do you ask more than one question in one item, for example, 'Is the website design pleasing and clear?' A website can be pleasing and yet unclear. Ask one question at a time.
- *Clarity*: Does the question make each alternative explicit? It is important that each alternative is unique and well defined.

- *Non-threatening*: Is the wording objectionable, loaded or slanted? Choose wording carefully to avoid offending the participant. Reword threatening items so that they do not elicit strong, negative reactions.

Decide how to order the items

Arrange items in an order that makes sense to the participants and facilitates easy movement through the questionnaire and thoughtful completion of the questions. Consider the following when planning the arrangement of your questionnaire (Lindgaard, 1994: 173–8).

Similar issues

If you have questions that deal with different issues, keep questions pertaining to the same issue together and separate from those of different issues. Use headings to identify each issue clearly.

Similar formats

After grouping together items about similar issues, keep questions of similar formats together. Number the questions and pages sequentially, and use plenty of white space to facilitate reading.

Be clear without being tedious

Remember that fewer participants will respond if a questionnaire appears to be long and tedious. Address this issue by placing easier questions at the beginning and follow questions that are difficult and about delicate issues with more routine questions.

Stay consistent with your objectives

Include only questions that will yield answers that you plan to use and that are consistent with your objectives. If you will not use the answers, do not use the question.

Use different methods of phrasing

When using a rating-scale type question, use different methods of phrasing questions so that respondents are encouraged to read and think about each question. Questions that are all phrased positively can produce automatic responses from respondents. Try adding some negatively phrased questions.

Use cards to help design the layout

To help design the layout of the questionnaire, write each question on a separate card; lay out these cards to try different arrangements.

Pilot and revise the questionnaire

When you have completed the arrangement of the questionnaire, and it meets with the approval of the development team, conduct a pilot test. A pilot test or trial run of the questionnaire and the distribution method is necessary for a final check of your methods and design. Use representatives of the target population. This is a simulation of the actual survey, so you need to distribute and collect the survey in the same manner that you will use with the actual survey. For example, if you have decided to distribute the survey using an e-mail message with an embedded link to a web-based survey, then use this method in the pilot test.

The objective of pilot testing is to search for problems with the distribution method, the clarity of the questions, the layout of the questionnaire, and the technology if your survey is computer-based. This is the time to check the responses to make certain you are generating information that will answer your questions and will satisfy the objectives of the study. Do not forget to check the responses for the ease of analysing the results. Can the format of the question be changed to make it easier to analyse?

After participants have completed the pilot, you can ask if they had any problems or can offer suggestions. You can also ask them if they did not understand what was meant by any of the questions or if they had problems choosing an answer from the given choices. You can revise the questionnaire based on the results of the pilot testing.

How do I distribute the questionnaire?

Select a sample of the target population

Usually your target population is too large to send the survey to the entire group so you have to select a sample, a smaller group, of the target population. Large representative samples are often used with mail surveys, drop-off surveys and e-mail surveys.

Some questionnaires need only a small sample. This might be true of group-administered and individually-administered questionnaires. For these cases you still should try to select participants who represent, at least in part, the target population. You can use a screening questionnaire to select participants who volunteer to participate. (For more information see the section on recruiting participants.)

Distribute the questionnaire

The method you use to distribute the questionnaire is dependent of the type of survey you have selected. Each has advantages and disadvantages. Your choice of distribution method will depend on the objectives of the survey, the sampling method, the participants, and the point in the development cycle when you use the questionnaire. Please see the section on 'questionnaires' for a more detailed description of the types of questionnaires and the methods of distribution.

How do I communicate the results?

The responses from participants are the data for the questionnaire. When you analyse the results, you are 'pulling the information together to make observations, conduct analyses, make interpretations, and draw conclusions' (Kasunic, 2005: 93).

For the screening questionnaires you do not need to communicate the results. The information is for your use when selecting a representative group of participants. For questionnaires that follow think aloud protocols, you simply tabulate the average response and report the findings within the final report of the usability testing activity. You might want to include a chart that shows the average response or display the results in a chart.

If you have used a longer questionnaire, you need to compile the results so that you can interpret the data and draw the conclusions that will be communicated in the final report. This step is easy if you are using a web-based survey and survey development software, as the data are automatically compiled. Pay attention to the questions that had few responses. This could indicate that the question was unclear, so interpret the results carefully.

When using a paper-based questionnaire, there are several steps before you can summarise the findings in a report. You need to code and compile the data, interpret the results, then the draw conclusions to be communicated in the final report (Kasunic, 2005: 94–107).

What are the advantages?

Questionnaires are fairly inexpensive and can be used individually or with large groups. They are an effective method of surveying large groups. They provide a means of quantifying the results. Attitude scales or multiple choice items are easy to analyse. Questionnaires are a quick method of generating a broad range of responses. They are free from investigator effects. The staff and faculty times are low.

What are the disadvantages?

The biggest disadvantage of questionnaires filled in remotely, such as mail or online surveys, is that the response rate is low. It is not unusual to expect a return rate for a mail survey to be around 25 per cent (Jordan, 1994: 451–60). The process is inflexible due to the static nature of the items.

The design of the questionnaire requires some expertise to create clearly worded and unbiased questions. They must be designed carefully because participants cannot gain additional information about a questionable item unless the questionnaire is administered in person or in a group (e.g. focus group). Mail and online questionnaires lack personal contact and are not well suited for open-ended essay-type items. Questionnaires are most effective when conducting a short survey.

Interviews

A second major category of surveys is the interview. Interviews, which can be conducted as a one-to-one activity or as a group activity, are a method of talking directly to the participant(s) to gather information. They often yield more detailed, in-depth information than questionnaires and provide the opportunity to probe the response further. To ensure that you receive accurate and complete information, there are four factors to consider when planning and conducting interviews (Lindgaard, 1994: 150):

- Does the participant have access to the information? If the participant neither knows the answer nor has access to the information, the questions will not be answered correctly.

- Does the participant understand the question? To provide a complete answer, the participant needs to understand what the interviewer wants to know and the level of detail that is requested.

- Are the participants motivated to provide the requested information? If the participant is tired, the interview is longer than expected, or the questions are boring, too personal or unclear, the results might be inaccurate or incomplete.

- Do participants understand the reasons for the interview, how the data will be used, and their rights to privacy and confidentiality? Understanding the nature of the research will motivate participants.

Interviews typically generate a broader range of responses than a questionnaire. They are good for getting subjective reactions, ideas, opinions and insights about issues (Usability First, 2005). They are useful in the process of designing library websites during participatory design to solicit ideas from the development team or target users, or to evaluate an existing website. The type of interview you use depends on the objectives of the evaluation. You can use person-to-person interviews, contextual interviews, or group interviews, known as focus groups. These will be discussed in the following sections.

Person-to-person interview

What is a person-to-person interview?

In a person-to-person interview, questions are posed directly to the participant. Although they can be conducted by telephone, person-to-person interviews in usability evaluation are usually where the researcher and participant meet face-to-face. Interviews, which follow a standardised script, can be structured, semi-structured or unstructured (Jordan, 1998: 68–70).

Structured interview

In structured interviews participants respond to a question by choosing from a set of given choices, such as in a multiple choice question; provide a response, such as in short answer questions; or choose from within a given range, such as with attitude scales (e.g. Likert scale). Although researchers need to have a thorough understanding of the issues in order to design a structured interview, the advantage is that the responses can be systematically quantitatively analysed.

Semi-structured interview

Semi-structured interviews are less controlled than structured interviews. The interview script is based on some knowledge of the issues. General and open-ended questions focused on an issue or feature of the target website encourage discussion, thus yielding a broader response from participants than from structured interviews. Interviewers can prompt participants for more information and respond to their questions and comments, while still providing them the option of addressing their own concerns. Because interview scripts are consistent among participants and cover the same range of issues, the results can be systematically analysed.

Unstructured interview

Unstructured interviews are comprised of general, open-ended questions and might be appropriate when the researcher has little knowledge of the issues. Open-ended questions offer the participant more opportunity to take the discussion towards issues they consider important. Although they can be difficult and time-consuming to analyse, the broad nature of the interview yields a wide range of responses and offers an opportunity to investigate ideas, attitudes and issues without restraint.

What is the objective?

The objective of a person-to-person interview is to generate information that can be useful in the design, development, and use of the current or proposed website. It is useful for generating ideas, opinions and reactions from participants. A person-to-person interview can be used to evaluate an existing website or to gain information that might be helpful in designing a new website.

Who are the participants?

The participants can be any member of the stakeholder groups, including content experts, developers and members of the target population.

How long will it take?

The length of time is dependent on the objective of the evaluation, the number of participants, and how you report the findings. You need to determine the objectives of your interview and write a script that will generate discussion that addresses your objectives. You need to recruit the participants and schedule the interviews. Activities to analyse and report the results of the interviews can include transcribing and coding the interview responses, analysing the data, interpreting the analysis, and communicating the findings. The total time for this evaluation method can be anywhere from a few days to several weeks, depending on the number of participants and the type and length of the interviews.

The length of time for a scheduled interview depends on the type of interview and the length of questions. A semi-structured interview to determine the needs and expectations of prospective users preceding the development of the website can take one to two hours. If an interview follows think aloud protocols and is designed to evaluate the website that was just tested, the length of time might be 10 or 15 minutes.

What materials do you need?

To conduct an interview, you need a script, recruiting materials, scheduling materials and incentives. If the interview is audio-taped, taping equipment and consent forms are necessary. (For more information see the section on recruiting participants.)

Where are they held?

Person-to-person interviews are most effective when conducted in a quiet place that offers some privacy. If the interviews are audio-recorded, a place that is protected from outside or extraneous noises offers the least interference.

What are the advantages?

Person-to-person interviews encourage more in-depth responses from participants than do questionnaires. Unlike in a focus group, there are no other participants to influence the outcome of a person-to-person interview; in addition, they can be used at any stage of the development cycle (Brinck et al., 2002: 85). With the interviewer present during the session, participants can ask for clarification of questions, decreasing the likelihood of misinterpretations. An effective interview script may require less preparation time than is necessary for a questionnaire (Jordan, 1998: 69).

What are the disadvantages?

Person-to-person interviews can be time-consuming and labour-intensive, making this method more costly than, for instance, a questionnaire. Because an interviewer is present, the participants might be less likely to give opinions that might be regarded as extremely negative, resulting in responses that lean towards more moderate levels.

Contextual interview

What is a contextual interview?

The contextual interview has roots in the fields of psychology, anthropology and sociology (Tec-Ed Services, 2008b). Typically in a contextual interview, you 'go where the customer works, observe the customer as he or she works, and talk to the customer about the work' (Beyer and Holtzblatt, 1998: 41). When designing or redesigning a university or college library website, observing and talking with users can take place either in the library or the user's office or workplace (which is often on campus). Assuming the target audience is local, the observation and interviews could even be conducted at both sites.

Facilitators observe participants as they operate the website as they would during a normal work session, or complete a set of prewritten task scenarios. Most often in usability evaluation the participants complete a set of task scenarios, similar to a think aloud protocol session.

The facilitator and often a note-taker observe and take notes about the user's actions and verbal responses. 'Because it is so difficult for people to describe exactly what they do and how much time they spend on various activities, the best way to find out is to become part of the procedures' (Lindgaard, 1994: 98) using participant observation methods. You have the opportunity to observe the environment, the hardware they use, the space, and any additional resources they use, such as notebooks and forms.

What is the objective?

Observations in the field are the best way to attempt to understand how people use the target website in normal situations and 'for describing, understanding and asking questions about what users are doing' (Lindgaard, 1994: 99–100). Observations of participants as they complete tasks relevant to their work in an everyday situation inform the task analysis and task scenarios (Mayhew, 1999: 69). In addition, observing users in an everyday situation generates information about the social environment, the availability of people to offer help, and the context of the work environment (Usability.gov, year unknown: b). Facilitators can observe any additional resources participants access to complement the services of the website, what steps they follow, and what data are required to complete the tasks.

For a newly designed interface, you need an operating interface or website to conduct contextual interviews, so the technique is most appropriate in the late stages of a project after the interface or website has been developed, although for a redesign effort, the method can be used early in the development cycle to detect usability problems in the current system.

Who are the participants?

Participants in contextual interviews are representatives of the target users. For a library website, they would include students, faculty, staff or others who use the library's collections and/or services.

How long will it take?

The length of time to complete an evaluation using contextual interviews is dependent on the objective and scope of the evaluation, the type of activity, and the number of participants. The total time can be anywhere from a few days to several weeks.

You need to determine the objectives of your interview. When using task scenarios, you need to write a script, develop scenarios, and decide on tasks that will generate information that will meet your objectives. Then you need to recruit the participants and schedule the interviews, transcribe and code the interview responses, analyse the data, interpret the analysis, and communicate the results.

When using task scenarios, expect each session to take about one to two hours for completion of tasks and for the discussion. This does not include travelling time. Allow time for introductions, observations, completion of tasks and discussion.

What materials do you need?

You need an operating interface or website and a paper prototype or mock-up of the interface. When using task scenarios, you need a written script of the set of task scenarios that participants are asked to complete. If the sessions are electronically recorded, you need audio or videotape equipment.

In order to recruit participants, facilitators will need recruitment posters, letters and/or e-mails scheduling materials (e.g. letter or e-mail, schedule of participants, thank you letters or e-mails), incentives, and consent forms when applicable. (For more information see the section on recruiting participants.)

Where are they held?

They are held in the user's workplace, home or office; when evaluating a library website, they can be held in the library as participants use library software or the library's website to find information.

What are the advantages?

Contextual interviews are most applicable when you need to understand users' work context. Compared with other methods, contextual interviews afford the best opportunity to observe the user operating the website in a normal setting. Observing users in their own setting is less formal than think aloud protocols and provides feedback about usability problems and environmental influences or needs.

What are the disadvantages?

The presence of the researcher during observations can affect how the user operates the website. When the contextual interviews do not use task scenarios, observing users as they conduct their own work limits the type of behaviour that is observed and lacks the consistency that is offered by task scenarios. Data analysis can be complicated and time-consuming.

How do you conduct a contextual interview?

When completing task scenarios during contextual interviews, the process is similar to think aloud protocols. The main difference is that contextual interviews take place in the user's typical work environment. Based on a task analysis, you need to develop a series of task scenarios. After recruiting representative users and scheduling the sessions, you conduct the sessions. The sessions can be video or audio-recorded. (For more information see the section on think aloud protocols.)

What is the role of the facilitator?

Facilitators welcome participants, explain the procedure, and create a non-threatening atmosphere while remaining neutral. The facilitator times the activity, observes the participant completing the tasks, and records any problems, as well as other materials the participant uses to complete the tasks. The facilitator encourages discussion, suggestions and comments.

How do you report the results?

Your notes from your observations and the comments from the participants are the data collected from a contextual interview. You need to summarise your observations of each interview and join the summaries in a complete report. Your report should summarise key issues: problems and the frequency of occurrence, materials that the participants used, and comments and suggestions.

The compilation and interpretation of data will be included in the written report. Depending on the length and purpose of the interviews, you can choose an informal quick report or a formal report to communicate the results. Because interviews are data-rich, it is not unusual to communicate the results in a formal report. To further illustrate a point you can include exact quotes from the participants.

Focus groups

What is a focus group?

A focus group is a non-empirical evaluation method that generates qualitative data. It is a moderated discussion with a group of representative stakeholders who discuss a particular issue related to the library website design or redesign effort. Rather than simply a group discussion, 'A genuine focus group is a focused group interview of six to twelve people, guided by a moderator and recorded for subsequent analysis' (Evaluation for Learning, 1999). Because focus groups involve only a small sample and the data are the transcripts of the discussion, 'focus group interviews do not generate quantitative information, and the results strictly speaking should not be generalised or "projected" to a larger population' (Usability Net, 2006a).

The group leader or moderator follows a pre-written, loosely structured script to promp more conversation or to direct the conversation around the topic of interest. The group discussion is recorded with hand-written notes and/or audio or videotaping and subsequently compiled and analysed to determine users' reactions, perceptions, ideas and thoughts regarding an aspect of the website, a new digital collection, or new library software or system.

Focus groups generate a broad range of qualitative feedback that provides an idea of participants' perceptions, their expectations, and their needs surrounding an issue (Brinck et al., 2002: 87). In a group discussion, participants' comments stimulate others to react or build on what other participants say. It is similar to brainstorming although generally more focused.

What is the objective?

The main objective of a focus group in user-centred design and usability evaluation is 'to discover what users want from the system' (Nielsen, 1997). Focus groups are useful when you need to explore subjective reactions, perceptions and views surrounding the target website. Focus groups can provide ideas that will help you to improve the usability, usefulness and design of the website.

Focus groups are useful at any stage of the development cycle, although because of the general nature of the feedback, they are most valuable in the early stages of development when a broad range of ideas and issues are useful to feed the design, to inform the user needs assessment, or to develop the task analysis (see the section on task analysis). Focus groups can also be used to inform the design or to elicit opinions regarding an already established website.

Although you can generate information using one focus group, often more than one group is scheduled to elicit feedback from more participants. Using more than one focus group will improve the validity of the study (Barnum, 2002: 45). 'A single focus group may be heavily biased by the mix of people involved, and you would never even know there was a problem unless you'd conducted a second group' (Brinck et al., 2002: 92). When you follow a consistent script among multiple focus groups, the discussion notes and transcripts can be combined and summarised into one report.

How do you create the discussion script?

A moderator guides the focus group, often using a prepared script to lead participants through the discussion. The purpose of the script is to guide and direct the conversation, trigger discussion, and keep the discussion on target. The discussion script begins with a welcome, introductions and a brief explanation of the topic of the discussion.

Begin the session with a general question or direction, something that is common to all participants and that encourages all to respond. This will help to create a more relaxed atmosphere for the discussion. For example, you might ask each participant to use one adjective or phrase to describe the topic of interest.

Slowly build to the main topics and key questions of the discussion. Use open-ended questions that stimulate a broad range of responses and avoid questions that can be answered with one or two words. When you have completed the discussion, summarise the main points and give participants an opportunity to add comments and suggestions. At the end of the session thank participants for their feedback and, if planned, distribute incentives.

What is the role of the moderator?

Usually each focus group has one moderator and often a note-taker. An important role of the successful group leader is to manage group dynamics (Jordan, 1998: 56; Brinck et al., 2002: 91). Not only do moderators keep the discussion focused on key points, but they also maintain a free-flowing discussion. The moderator introduces the session and draws all participants into the discussion. They remind participants that the opinions of all members are important, that there are no wrong answers, and that the purpose is to hear all opinions. The moderator manages the groups, enabling them to 'work cooperatively and effectively,' especially those who tend to control the discussion (Gaffney, 2000a). After each item or question, the moderator can summarise the opinions expressed by the group to make certain that the responses were all heard and interpreted as intended.

The focus group works best if the moderator remains neutral during the discussion (Evaluation for Learning, 2000). When moderators express an opinion, they run the risk of influencing others in the group who might be swayed to agree with them. A good method for moderators to

Where are they held?

Focus groups are held in a comfortable, neutral place that provides a quiet atmosphere conducive to discussion. Focus groups are often conducted at a round or oval table in a conference or meeting room.

Do you need a pilot test for the session?

While a full pilot test or trial run of the focus group is often helpful to gauge the length of time that will be needed for the session and the usefulness of the discussion script, a complete pilot test with multiple participants might be unrealistic considering the time and budget. If you are unable to complete a pilot test, then consider an abridged version of the pilot test. Include a representative user(s) who will respond to the discussion questions and follow with an interview to probe for problems.

An interview will let you know if the vocabulary is familiar to participants and if the questions are worded clearly and generate the type of information that you want. The abridged pilot test will also give you an idea of the length of time needed for a session. Based on the time for the pilot you can estimate how long the session will be with additional participants. You can revise your script based on the results of your pilot test.

How do you report the results?

You can report results in an informal or formal report. An informal report might include a brief summary of methods and a list of the key findings and recommendations. A formal report will be more detailed and describe the methods, the participants, and the key findings and recommendations.

Your notes and the transcript of the comments from the participants are the data collected from a focus group. Your report should summarise key problems and issues, the frequency of the occurrence, and the participants' comments and suggestions. Based on the summary of the focus group you are ready to make recommendations either for the design or redesign of the website. All of this will be included in the written report.

What are the advantages?

Focus groups are a good method of generating a broad range of attitudes, ideas or opinions from a diverse set of participants. Due to the loose structure of the focus group, ideas and issues might be raised that had not been previously considered by the development team. 'If one person raises an idea, then another person can build on the idea, and you can delve into far greater detail on some issues by following up lines of thought that the interviewer might not have even known to pursue' (Brinck et al., 2002: 85; Webcredible.co.uk, year unknown).

Although they can be used at any stage in the development cycle, this type of feedback is most useful in the early stages of website development to screen for 'potential usability pitfalls that need to be avoided' (Brinck et al., 2002: 56).

What are the disadvantages?

Focus groups generate ideas and opinions; they are not suitable to determine how users actually navigate the website, find information, or to evaluate the website or digital interface for usability problems. What people say is not necessarily consistent with their current or future

Table 3.2   Example – planning a focus group

Identify the problem, select the method	During the planning stage of the redesign of the library website, we needed to learn about potential users' expectations, needs, opinions, and suggestions about the current and targeted website. We used two focus groups, one for staff and faculty and one for undergraduate and graduate students, to generate a broad range of ideas and suggestions.
Pilot the activity	In two separate pilot sessions we asked a library staff person and a student worker to respond to the focus group questions. Based on the pilot, we revised the script to eliminate items that didn't generate useful information, rewrote items that were confusing, and edited the script to meet our time requirements.
Determine incentives	We offered each student participant a monetary incentive of $20, and beverages and snacks. The staff and faculty group were invited to a lunch for a group discussion.
Arrange for a room and refreshments	We used the library's fine and rare book collection room for the student group. Because we were serving food, we used a meeting room in a central building on campus for the staff/faculty group. Both rooms had large tables, were comfortable and pleasing, and had plenty of room to serve food and beverages.
Prepare materials	We created a demographic screening survey using an online survey website, a request e-mail, an acceptance e-mail, a reminder e-mail, and a thank you e-mail. We also created scheduling forms.
Prepare the script	The script started with a general item to warm up the group, something that generated a comment from everyone. For example, we asked, 'Tell me one adjective or phrase that comes to mind when you look at the home page'. We used questions that asked participants for their ideas or suggestions about the appearance, the categories, and the terminology. We then asked general questions about issues or problems they had or anticipated having with the website. The final item was a general question that asked for additional suggestions or comments.
Recruit participants	To generate a representative sample of about 8–10 for each group, we wrote an e-mail announcement that was posted on university electronic b-boards. In the e-mail, we included a link to a demographic survey, and asked volunteers to respond to the survey. We also wanted to include faculty, so we sent out an e-mail to several faculty members from various disciplines.
Select participants	Based on the responses to the demographic survey, we selected eight participants who represented the targeted population of users. We sent out a scheduling e-mail that contained the details of the session, description of the activity, location and date. We scheduled all participants
Reminder	The day before the session, we sent out reminders to all scheduled participants reminding them of the session date, time and place.
Prepare the room	The day of the session, we prepared the room, arranging seating and beverages and/or food. Each participant had the option to use name cards or place cards. In addition to note-taking, we used a flip chart to record the main ideas that were expressed.

behaviour (Norman, 1998). Although focus group feedback can be summarised quantitatively, due to its subjective nature, it is not good quantitative data.

There are some dangers that the group dynamics may be dominated by one or two participants; thus, a strong resourceful moderator is needed to guide the discussion and ensure that all are heard and that none dominate. The conversation, although guided, might focus on specific issues and avoid others that are either not of interest or which simply were not considered at the time.

Tables 3.2 and 3.3 provide examples of how a focus group might be planned and moderated.

Table 3.3   **Example – moderating a focus group session**

Welcome	We welcomed participants, explained the objective of the focus group, and what we would be doing.
Focus group discussion	Following the written script the moderator conducted the focus group. The moderator summarised the responses at the end of each item or question, e.g. 'To summarise, you feel that the current homepage is cluttered, has too many links, and that you need better or more familiar link names. Is that correct?'
Moderator's role	The moderator guided the session loosely following a script, encouraged all to talk (e.g. 'How do you feel about that, John?') or discouraged others from taking control of the session (e.g. 'We've heard your suggestions, how about you, Mary?')
Conclude session	The moderator thanked the participants for coming and distributed the incentives to the students.
Thank you notes	The following day we sent an e-mail or note thanking each participant for their contributions.

4

Designing the website – participatory design

To create a user-centred website, it is important that all stakeholders or stakeholder representatives, from content experts to target users, are involved in the design of the website or interface from the very beginning of the design and development cycle. They offer feedback concerning the site design from their own perspectives. Early in the project, content experts help to define the scope of the project and the structure of the content; designers provide feedback relative to the design and layout of the site; analysts, evaluators, and usability specialists provide feedback about the evaluation plan and usability guidelines; and target users provide feedback about the ease of use and usefulness of the site.

Though we are certain that feedback from many different stakeholders' perspectives is necessary to design and develop a user-centred website, the question remains about how to generate this feedback. The methods used are referred to as participatory design – quite literally, a group of diverse stakeholders participate in the design of the site.

Participatory design

Participatory design describes methods of inquiry that generate feedback from a diverse group of stakeholders about all aspects of website design and development. Sometimes referred to as participative inquiry, participatory design describes multiple methods that bring together stakeholders, most importantly representative users, to work towards developing a user-centred design (Rubin, 1994: 20).

This process is especially helpful for the designers and developers in the early stages of development when the focus is on the design. In other evaluation methods, designers and developers often work apart from other stakeholders. By involving representatives from various stakeholder groups, who bring their own perspectives to the discussion, key players in the website's development have a better understanding of the problems and issues related the design, thus enhancing the process (Kneifel and Guerrero, 2003: 407).

Because participants do not always know what they want, 'getting useful design information from prospective users is not just a matter of asking' (Gould and Lewis, 1985: 303). Specific methods produce useful information in the participatory design process. The methods are often similar to a focus group with the addition of activities that are designed to achieve specific objectives. They involve stakeholders in a hands-on manner to elicit direct feedback on development and design issues, for example, how the information should be grouped or what the interface should look like. Using stakeholder feedback early in the process can save time and effort. When feedback is collected late in the cycle design, redesign efforts are labour-intensive, more costly and time-consuming.

What is the objective?

The primary objective of participatory design is to gather feedback from all stakeholders to feed the design or redesign of an interface, website, software or system. A secondary but equally important objective is for members to learn from each other, therefore leading to a better understanding of the different perspectives of the problems and issues. As described by Gaffney (2000b), participatory design sessions:

- provide an opportunity for all stakeholders and target users to have a voice in the design of the system, increasing the probability of a more usable design;
- enable both technical and non-technical stakeholders to interact, enabling them to provide feedback and also have a greater understanding of their diverse perspectives;
- provide an opportunity to identify the issues using a highly-productive method.

Who are the participants?

Participatory design includes all stakeholders, that is, everyone who participates in the design, development, management and use of the website. In a university or college library, stakeholders can include content experts such as librarians and archivists, developers and designers, usability professionals, human factors researchers and representative users.

While participatory design sessions that include all stakeholder representatives in one meeting are an opportunity to learn about the perspectives of the diverse groups, they also risk affecting the responses. Some stakeholders might be concerned about offending others, for example, users concerned about offending designers and developers. To avoid this problem, multiple meetings are often scheduled that follow a similar format but with a subset of representative, but similar, stakeholders.

What are the advantages?

Participatory design methods are the best way to involve all representative stakeholders, especially representative users, in the design and development process early in the development cycle.

When used in the early stages of the development cycle, feedback gathered from these methods will contribute to the development of a user-centred website with the least amount of effort and cost.

What are the disadvantages?

The potential danger is that representative users can become so familiar with the interface design that they begin to think more like the design and development experts and less like target users (Rubin, 1994: 20). Participatory design requires additional time for stakeholders.

Bringing all stakeholders together in a meeting could affect the input from users who might be reluctant to provide ideas or feedback when developers are present, either because they do not want to appear critical or are afraid of appearing uninformed.

What methods are used?

Participatory design is effective with group activities such as affinity diagramming, card sorting, and prototyping. These methods are described more fully in the following section.

Affinity diagramming

Affinity diagramming is a useful method of grouping and understanding information, organising concepts and ideas, and analysing ideas (Gaffney, 2000c). Similar to brainstorming. where participants offer suggestions, comments and ideas in a free-flowing manner, with affinity diagramming the ideas are written rather than submitted verbally. In a group session, participants are encouraged to write issues on sticky notes – one issue per note. Issues are anything related to the target website and can be about such things as design, content links, navigation or help. Figure 4.1 gives an example of an affinity diagram.

After allowing time for participants to collect their thoughts and complete their notes, each participant, in turn, reads their notes and places them in an existing or new group on a wall, white board, or bulletin board. Once the first note has been placed, other participants can place

Figure 4.1   Example of an affinity diagram

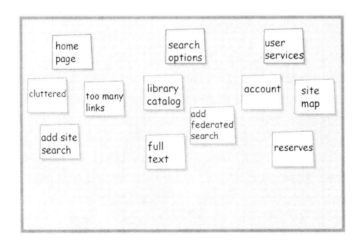

related notes. Categories can be labelled in advance, labelled during the placement of notes, or after all notes have been added.

After all notes have been placed, allow time for discussion and movement of notes from one category to another. Encourage discussion surrounding the placement of the notes. Because the placement is arbitrary, notes can be moved into other categories, to a new category, or to more than one category. For additional information to report in the results, observe and record the discussion surrounding the placement of notes. Observe when there is agreement or disagreement surrounding an issue. The discussion and categories of notes will be the data that you analyse for the report.

When participants are satisfied that notes are in appropriate categories, you can ask them to complete an activity to prioritise the notes (Snyder, 2003). Each participant will choose the top three items in each category that they feel are the most important. Participants can also be asked to choose the top three categories that are the most important.

What is the objective?

Affinity diagramming is used to elicit feedback from owners, developers, users and other stakeholders about categorising, prioritising and understanding information on your website. It can be used to identify, organise and analyse issues related to website design and development. It is also useful for organising large amounts of qualitative data similar to that which results from contextual inquiry or brainstorming ideas (Barnum, 2002: 250). This method is often useful during the planning and design stage of website development.

Who are the participants?

Participants need to represent stakeholders. For a library website, participants can include target users, reference librarians, designers, developers, and human factors and usability experts. A group of six to ten works well.

What is the role of the faciltator?

The faciltator welcomes participants, introduces the activity, and describes the activity. During the session the faciltator responds to questions, reminds participants of the types of issues, and encourages all to participate and none to take control. Faciltators encourage participants to read notes aloud, place one note at a time, and remind others to place similar notes. They determine when the session ends, trying not to extend the session past the point when participants are tired or bored. Faciltators also need to pay attention to what is happening and record the discussion around the issues.

The process is sometimes confusing and difficult for participants, although by the end of the activity, they usually understand the value. As Barnum (2002: 251) suggests, you should consider that that participants in this activity may go through the following stages:

- they might become overwhelmed, or confused about how to begin;

- after becoming familiar with the process, they might do gross categorisation;

- they might become frustrated with the details of categorisation and unclear about the rationale of the process;

- they understand that the process is valuable for transforming information into meaningful concepts.

How long will it take?

The amount of time to plan and conduct affinity diagramming will vary depending on the objectives of your evaluation, the depth of the discussion, the number of groups and participants, and the type of report you complete. The entire process can take anywhere from several days to several weeks.

You need to determine the objectives, write a script and develop materials to focus the activity, as well as recruit and schedule participants. You might decide that in order to generate optimal representative feedback, you need to conduct more than one group. These planning and preparation activities will take several days. Add more time for multiple groups and more participants. If you are planning more than one group, you need to allow time for all group sessions; these might take one to two hours for each session.

You need time to analyse and interpret the data and write the final report. This could take several days to a few weeks depending on the scope of the activity and the type of report. If the objective of affinity diagramming is to gain information that informs the design of an interface, allow time to make recommendations for the revisions or to revise the prototype.

What materials do you need?

Physical materials include sticky notes, pens and a pad for each participant. Use a different colour of sticky notes for the group labels. You also need a script for the moderator and materials to focus the activity. This might be screenshots of the target website, a prototype, or the actual functioning website. The moderator might need a flip chart, notepad or laptop to record observations and the discussion surrounding the issues.

Where are they held?

Group sessions can be conducted in a private space with a table that has plenty of space for participants to write their notes. You need a flat wall space (bulletin board or white board) to place notes.

How do you report the results?

Summarise the data

The data from affinity diagramming are the groups or categories of sticky notes that were placed by the participants. Data also include the moderator's notes and observations of the verbal discourse and behaviour of the participants as they completed their tasks. These data provide the basis for the categorisation and analysis used to prepare the summary report.

Summarise the notes, categories and category headings, and the issues surrounding each category including the moderator's observations. Include priorities of issues and feelings of participants (frustration, agreement or non-agreement).

Write the report

First decide if you will write a formal or informal report. An informal report might include a few sentences that describe the process and participants. Include a list of the findings, the primary groupings, the issues and the recommendations.

A formal report includes a more detailed description of the methods used, the participants, the process and the findings. Important information to include in the summary report consists of a short description of the procedures, the participants' demographics, a summary of the data, in this case, the groupings and issues, and the recommendations by the participants.

The objective is to simplify the wealth of issues and information by similarity and main concerns so that the information is easily managed. The groupings can be reported in the form of a chart or in a spreadsheet.

How to use the information

It is best if the results can be used quickly to address the design of the website. A follow-up session should be conducted to discuss methods to address any issues raised (Gaffney, 2000c). Remember that the small number of participants is not enough to be a true representation of the population of targeted users; the groupings can therefore be considered arbitrary. Use this information with other relevant information when designing the end-user interface or website.

What are the advantages?

Affinity diagramming is an inexpensive, effective and relatively simple method for including all stakeholders in the process of interface, website or system design. It is a means of sorting large amounts of information, identifying issues and determining priorities (Usability Net, 2006b).

What are the disadvantages?

The process can be long and tiring. Because it uses a small group, this method will not represent the general population of users. Consider the results as arbitrary and use the results of affinity diagramming with other methods. Tables 4.1 and 4.2 provide examples of how an affinity diagramming session might be planned and facilitated.

Table 4.1 Example – planning an affinity diagramming session

Identify the problem	We defined the problem, that is, how we would focus the session. For example, during the planning stage of the redesign of the library website, we needed to generate student views of the issues related to the website including content, usability, navigation, and usefulness. We focused on the homepage.
Prepare materials	We assembled pens and sticky notes (one for each participant), using different colours of notes for category headings. We included note-taking materials for the moderator. We prepared other materials to focus the activity (e.g. screenshot of the homepage). We arranged for beverages/refreshments and incentives, and brought extra materials.
Determine incentives	Student participants were offered a monetary incentive of $20, in addition to the opportunity to contribute to the design of the website.
Arrange for a room	We used the library conference room. It had a large table that provided space for participants to write notes and plenty of wall space to arrange notes. The room was quiet and private.
Recruit participants	We recruited a representative sample of students by posting an e-mail announcement on university electronic bulletin boards that are frequented by students. We asked volunteers to respond to the e-mail. The e-mail included a few demographic questions that we used to screen and select a representative group. We also asked librarians for recommendations of students and student workers.
Send out the 'acceptance' letter	We selected representative participants based on responses to the e-mail and sent an 'acceptance' letter to each with details of the sessions and scheduling information.
Remind participants	A couple of days before the session we e-mailed all scheduled participants reminding them of the session date, time and place.
Prepare the room	The day of the session we prepared the room arranging materials, seating and beverages.

Table 4.2	Example – facilitating an affinity diagramming session
Welcome	We welcomed participants with introductions, described the objective of the session, and gave instructions on how to complete the activity.
Distribute the materials	We gave each participant a sticky note pad and placed other sticky note pads of different colours on the table for the category headings. Each participant had a copy of the screen display that would be used in the target website. We began the activity by asking participants to write down one issue per note about the target website. We gave them some examples and answered questions.
Place notes	When most participants had completed their notes, the facilitator asked one participant at a time to place their notes on the wall, trying to keep similar issues in the same category. When a note was placed, she asked if anyone had something similar and then added it to the category. After all items were placed, the facilitator, with the help of participants, labelled categories.
Observation and note-taking	The facilitator observed participants as they completed the task, noted difficulties they were having, and offered help as needed. She also recorded the discussion and her observations.
Summarise the activity	When all notes had been placed, the facilitator read each group of notes aloud and asked if anyone thought that a note should be moved. Some notes were placed in more than one category.
Conclude session	When participants had completed the task and the discussion was concluded, the facilitator collected the materials. She thanked the participants for coming and distributed the incentives.
Thank you	The following day we sent an e-mail thanking each participant for their contributions

Card sorting

What is card sorting?

Card sorting is a simple and effective method of sorting predetermined website-related information (e.g. tasks, documents and links) into meaningful categories, lists or groups based on the perspective of end-users. Participants organise cards labelled with names of content information. Like other participatory design activities, card sorting brings actual users into the design process, giving them a sense of involvement and an opportunity to offer their perspective.

Card sorting can be completed as an open card sort or a closed card sort (Mark Boulton Design, year unknown: a). In an open card sort, participants sort cards into categories that make sense to them and which they label with their own category titles. In a closed card sort, participants sort cards using predetermined categories. By encouraging participants to think out loud during the activity, their verbal discussion and suggestions can be used to learn more about the mental models of how they interpret and use the information.

Card sorting can be conducted as an individual activity or a group activity. That is, individuals can sort a set of cards into categories or a group of participants can work together to sort a set of cards into categories. An advantage to conducting the technique as a group activity is that you have an opportunity to observe their actions and record their dialogue as they try to determine logical groupings (Robertson, 2001). In addition, groups can effectively manage more cards and categories because they are helping each other.

Card sorting can be a time-consuming and difficult task if using a large assortment of cards, so choose a section of the website interface that will keep the cards to a workable number (e.g. 20–45, but ideally no more than 30 cards). Groups can, of course, manage more cards than individuals.

Do not forget to pilot this activity with someone who is unfamiliar with your website, and note the time needed to complete the task and any difficulties they might experience.

What is the objective?

Card sorting is used to learn how potential users expect information to be organised, whether terminology for names and category titles is familiar, and the importance of the item to the page or group (Information Services and Technology, year unknown). 'Card sorting generates an overall structure for your information, as well as suggestions for navigation, menus, and possible taxonomies' (Maurer and Warfel, 2004). Based on users' expectations and feedback, this activity provides information about how to organise the website information, what users expect to find in content areas, page and website navigation, and page and website content.

Who are the participants?

The participants for card sorting are representative members of the targeted population of users with diverse characteristics such as computer expertise, year (e.g. freshman), and discipline. Although the most important group of participants is the end-user population, participants can also include any representative of the various groups of stakeholders, for example, the content experts, the designers and developers, and the usability specialists. Each group provides a different perspective.

Card sorting can be an individual activity (each individual sorts a set of cards) or a group activity (a group of three sort a set of cards). When completing the activity with individuals, you need about six to ten participants. They can complete the activity in one session or multiple sessions. If it is a group activity, then you need about 15 participants who will work in groups of three. You have one facilitator to guide the session and an observer or note-taker for each group.

How long will it take?

The amount of time for this type of evaluation will depend on the objectives of the evaluation, the number of cards participants will be sorting, the number of participants, the type of sessions (individual or group activity), and the type of report. The entire process can take several days to a several weeks.

You need to determine the objectives and scope of your evaluation, the content of the categories and cards, and how you will conduct the activity (individuals or in a group). You can schedule multiple sessions for different groups of stakeholders or for different participants to complete the activity, or you might schedule each participant separately. The method you choose will affect the time needed to complete the activity. You need to recruit and schedule participants (see the section on recruiting participants). The planning, preparation and scheduling will take several days.

You need to allow one to two hours for the session; group activities will take longer due to the discussion during sorting. The goal is to keep the actual card sorting activity to about one hour. If your pilot session is longer than one hour, consider decreasing the number of cards. You need to allow time for welcomes, instructions, card sorting, discussion and closing the session. You need time to compile, interpret and summarise the data, and communicate the findings.

How do you complete a card sorting activity?

Several steps are recommended to complete card sorting (Mark Boulton Design, year unknown: a; Usability Net, 2006c; Usability.gov, year unknown: c). Decide on the content area for your focus and create a set of cards. They can be items that are on the current website, or you can create a set of items based on your previous knowledge or input from the library content experts. Create a separate set of cards for the category headings (optional).

On the back of each card write a unique number. For prioritising, you can write a question on the back that asks participants to rate the priority of the item or the group. Shuffle each set of cards and band the sets – the content items and the headings (for closed card sort). Include blank cards in the sets. By labelling a blank card with a name used on another card, participants can place the same item in different groups. They can also use a blank card to add an item to the category or to change the category heading.

During the session, after instructions and a few examples, pass out the cards. If it is a closed card sorting, instruct participants to lay out the header cards and then to place all other cards in the appropriate group. If it is an open card sorting, instruct participants to place similar items together. Participants will create the heading cards after the sort is completed. Encourage participants to think out loud to voice their confusion, frustration or suggestions. Remind participants to prioritise the item using the rating on the back or by writing comments.

What is the role of the facilitator?

The facilitator introduces the session and guides the activity. During the card sorting, the facilitator and the note-takers should take notes about what participants are saying, what problems they have, which cards have been moved multiple times, or which cards seem confusing to participants. Facilitators remain neutral during the card sorting. You can use a digital camera to keep a reliable record of the resulting card sorting arrangement.

What materials do you need?

For each participant and the facilitator and note-takers you need one set of labelled white index cards and one set of blank index cards. You also need pens, a box of rubber bands to join groups of cards, and plenty of extras of everything. Bring materials for note-taking and incentives (optional). You need recruitment and scheduling materials, the script that the facilitator will use to guide the session, and notes for thanking participants.

Where are they held?

You need a room that has tables large enough for participants to spread out and sort their set of cards. The room should be private and offer a quiet and pleasing atmosphere that is conducive to discussion.

How do you report the results?

Compile and summarise the data

Data for the session are the observation notes, the participants' comments, the cards in each category, and the labels for the categories. To analyse the results of card sorting, start by placing participants' category groups and suggested names on a table or attached to a bulletin board, groups intact, to better observe and detect patterns. Look for common occurrences or problems with terminology, for example (Mark Boulton Design, year unknown: b; Maurer and Warfel, 2004; Tec-Ed Services, 2008c):

- item, group or category names that appear frequently;
- items, groups or categories that are difficult to name;
- content that usually appears together;
- content that often appears in many different groups;
- unfamiliar terminology or names;
- how users want the information grouped – by subject, process or type;
- number of menu items in each group;
- perceived importance of the item;
- differences among user groups.

Write the report

Important information to include in the summary report consists of a short description of the procedures, the participants' demographics, summary of the data (in this case, the main categories and items), and the recommendations by the participants. Indicate their primary concerns or priorities. The objective is to simplify the discussion so that it can be meaningful and useful.

How to use the information

With this information, you are better able to determine group types and group names. The issues and suggestions related to items and categories can inform the decisions about the terminology used on your website. The information about the perceived importance of items and confusion or issues surrounding other items will inform the inclusion or placement decisions for the website. The results of the card sorting can be used to design a logical (to users) set of lists and categories as well as clear terminology.

What are the advantages?

Card sorting is cost-effective, takes relatively little time, and generates feedback from potential users regarding logical groupings of website items.

What are the disadvantages?

Analysing the results can be time-consuming and sometimes difficult, especially if using a large number of cards. Tables 4.3 and 4.4 provide examples of how a card sorting session might be planned and moderated.

Prototyping

Twenty years of usability engineering experience uniformly indicates that the biggest improvements in user experience come from gathering usability data as early as possible. (Nielsen, 1995: 88–89, 97)

Traditional methods of building software, that is, collecting user information, designing and building the software, and presenting it to users for trial and feedback, fail to meet user requirements for three reasons: users are not good at communicating what they want; even when developers design software according to users' specifications, users have problems with the software ('that's what I said but not what I want'); and often users do not represent all user groups (Hakim and Spitzer, 2000: 47–8). The solution is to use prototypes of the software early and throughout development to improve communication with users, to introduce alternative designs, and to learn about user requirements.

Table 4.3	Example – planning for a card sorting session

Identify the problem	We needed to decide what links will be included on the library website homepage and how they should be grouped.
Prepare materials	We identified a set of links and group headings based on suggestions from librarians and the existing homepage links. We wrote each item on separate white index cards. We wrote the group headings on coloured index cards. Keeping the group heading cards separate from the link name cards, we shuffled both sets of cards. On the back of each card we wrote a unique number for identification. To better understand how participants prioritise the items, we added to the back of the card: 'Rank the importance of this item (low/medium/high)'. We made two sets of labelled cards (one for the links and one for the headings) for each participant, the facilitator and note-taker – each set was contained by a rubber band. We included extra materials – labelled card packets, rubber bands, blank cards and pens.
Determine incentives	Each participant was offered a monetary incentive of $20, in addition to providing the opportunity to contribute to the design of the website.
Pilot the activity	We tried this activity with one or two volunteers who were not familiar with the website. We timed the activity and interviewed participants after they completed the sort. We revised as needed.
Arrange for a room and refreshments	We scheduled the library conference room, which had a large table that provided space for participants to spread out cards. We arranged for beverages and snacks.
Recruit participants	To generate a representative sample, we posted an e-mail announcement on university electronic bulletin boards that were frequented by students. Volunteers responded to a computer-based demographic survey by clicking on a link embedded in the e-mail.
Send out the 'acceptance' letter	We selected representative participants based on responses to the survey. We then sent out an 'acceptance' letter to each with details of the sessions and with scheduling information.
Remind participants	The day before the session we e-mailed all scheduled participants reminding them of the session date, time and place.
Prepare the room	The day of the session we organised the room arranging seating and preparing for beverages and snacks. We made name cards for participants and for the facilitator and note-takers.

A prototype is a draft copy of the proposed website. Prototyping is a method of gathering usability information beginning early in the website development cycle and throughout the development. 'A prototype is often the best way to gather feedback from users while you are still planning and designing your website' (Usability.gov, year unknown: d). It is a quick way to find out if you are on the right path with your plans and design.

Table 4.4   Example – facilitating a card sorting session

Welcome	The facilitator welcomed participants, explained why they were there, and how to complete the activity.
Pass out the materials	The facilitator passed out the materials and instructed participants about the purpose of the activity. She showed participants an example of how to complete the activity using her sets of cards. She reminded them of the information on the back of each card (prioritising the item).
Observation and note-taking	The facilitator and note-takers observed participants as they completed the task, noting any difficulties they were having. She encouraged participants to think out loud.
Conclude session	When participants completed the task, we banded their cards together and collected the materials. We thanked the participants for coming and distributed the incentives.
Thank you	The following day we sent an e-mail thanking each participant for their contributions

Prototypes are used to collect information that feeds the design and tests the usability. They can be developed to serve many objectives – 'to discover or refine user requirements, inspire or explore design ideas, share or co-develop designs with user participants, make a precise test of specific open issues, and share or deploy early implementation efforts' (Rosson and Carroll, 2001: 198).

The primary purpose of prototypes in usability evaluation and user-centred design is to look for problems or issues. This is why early use of prototypes before coding has begun will save time and money. The prototype design ranges from low-fidelity, primitive prototypes such as paper prototypes (hand-drawn designs of website pages) to more sophisticated, high-fidelity, dynamic prototypes such as a functioning prototype of the proposed website pages. The value of low-fidelity versus high-fidelity prototypes to generate useful and accurate usability feedback is not without some controversy. However, based on the results of several studies, both types of prototype have been found to produce useful usability information (Rudd, Stern and Isensee, 1996: 76–85; Virzi, 1996: 236–43; Sefelin, Tscheligi and Giller, 2003: 778–9; Baily, 2005).

Prototypes are used throughout the development cycle. 'Designers often sketch on paper early in the design process in order to quickly explore design ideas and to keep from focusing on low level details too early in the process' (Newman and Landay, 2000: 274). Later in the development, more sophisticated prototypes are used for early usability testing as part of an iterative design cycle. The development stage when prototypes are used will affect what type of prototype to use.

Many variations of prototypes fall between crude paper and pencil drawings (low-fidelity) and sophisticated, functional prototypes (high-fidelity). This section describes prototyping in user-centred design.

Low-fidelity, paper prototyping

What is paper prototyping?

A paper prototype is a draft of the proposed website created on paper. It can be as simple as a black and white hand drawing of the proposed website pages. A more detailed draft using applications such as Microsoft PowerPoint, Microsoft Access or Adobe Illustrator can be used to create a more sophisticated low-fidelity prototype using colour, icons, buttons and fonts. The primary distinction from high-fidelity prototypes is that low-fidelity prototypes are not functioning websites.

Before designing paper prototypes, the development team determines the objectives and the desired functionality of the website, and defines the target user groups and their requirements. The information collected from users and other stakeholders feeds the design of an early prototype. The design of paper prototypes has several characteristics (Snyder, 2001):

- They can be rough, hand-drawn sketches. When used in activities with participants, words can be read aloud, although not explained.

- They can use words rather than icons. Images can be represented using labelled boxes, for example, a box labelled 'logo'.

- They can be drawn in black and white so that participants can focus on the design. Colour can be added later.

- They can have components that vary in size in the sketches although will not vary in the actual website. You can explain to participants about the difference in sizes or in the line and page lengths.

Paper prototypes are often created by the designers or usability personnel; however, because some small projects do not have the specialists that larger projects or organisations might have, prototypes can be designed by anyone involved in the project. Representative stakeholders are brought together for a group discussion of the proposed website using paper prototypes to focus the discussion. Group discussions can include all stakeholders in one meeting or smaller groups of stakeholders in multiple meetings.

What is the objective?

The objective of paper prototyping is to inform the design of the website beginning early in the development cycle and continuing to the final website design. Paper prototypes are used as a focus of discussion in order to generate feedback about the design, usability and usefulness of the proposed website design. These 'studies can save a great deal of time, effort and money by enabling different ideas to be shown and user tested before a particular approach is settled on' (Lindgaard, 1994: 93).

In the early stages of design, the use of a rough sketch of the website in a participatory design session encourages discussion and questions (Rosson and Carroll, 2001: 201). Paper prototypes can be used in a focus group or affinity diagramming involving all representative stakeholders. A facilitator leads the discussion, drawing attention to key aspects of the website design such as the terminology, navigation links and appearance.

Paper prototypes can also be used to conduct usability testing. Moderators can set up a series of scenarios and ask users to indicate how they would complete the tasks. Because the design is on paper, users will point to the link. Facilitators will then show another page of the prototype and ask the user to continue the task. The process continues until all tasks are completed.

Who are the participants?

When paper prototyping is part of participatory design, the participants can include all stakeholders. Stakeholders include administrators, project leaders, content experts, usability personnel, human factors researchers, designers, developers and representative users – everyone who is involved in the development and use of the website.

Representatives of all groups can meet in one meeting or groups can meet separately in several meetings. Bringing all stakeholders together in the same meeting may influence the responses (Jordan, 1998: 57). Users might be reluctant to voice criticism in front of the developers and designers for fear of hurting their feelings or of appearing uninformed. Others may feel that it is in the interest of the developers to hear all concerns so that they will be better able to address problems.

Determining who to include in your meetings might be better decided based on the scheduling needs and desires of the stakeholders. After the meetings, it is important that all designs are discussed with developers before presenting them to the end-users to make certain that the proposed design meets with the allotted budget and time.

How long will it take?

The length of time needed for the evaluation activity depends on which method is used (see individual methods). The length of time for the entire process depends on the number of pages in the interface and the number and types of activities used to develop and test the design. The length of time can vary from a few weeks to several weeks.

You need time to create the prototype, conduct the evaluation activity, redesign the prototype based on feedback, and then to repeat the process until the prototype meets with stakeholder approval. The design of the prototype can be completed within a few days depending on the sophistication of the design (e.g. hand-drawn or more sophisticated application-assisted illustration).

What materials do you need?

The simplest form of paper prototypes can be completed using pencil, paper and scissors. More sophisticated drawings can be created using software such as Adobe Illustrator or Microsoft Publisher, PowerPoint or Access. You need a set of materials for the facilitator, the note-taker and each participant.

If the session is conducted as a group activity, you need a set of screen displays for all participants. You can present the prototypes on individual sheets of paper or in a booklet that includes questions and comments on the same page. Either way, you need a set for the moderator, the note-taker and each participant. The prototypes can also be shown as slides in a PowerPoint presentation.

As in other evaluation methods, you need all or some of the following: a script, a consent form, audio or videotaping materials (optional), recruitment and scheduling materials, other correspondence materials, and incentives.

What are the advantages?

'Paper prototyping is one of the fastest and cheapest techniques you can employ in a design process' (Nielsen, 2003b). Because paper prototypes are simple to design, easy to revise, and take little time, the process is inexpensive. These can be used to find serious problems early in the development process before the actual coding is begun. When usability evaluation is conducted with a live website later in the development cycle, problems found can take more time to fix and are more expensive to address. Paper prototyping can generate usability feedback throughout the development cycle, for example, after usability problems are found in the primary navigation, revisions can be evaluated by using rough sketches of alternatives in brief usability testing sessions.

What are the disadvantages?

Although usability testing can be simulated using paper prototypes, such simulations cannot provide the same level of target user feedback as observing users completing tasks using a functional website.

How do you use paper prototyping?

Paper prototypes can be used in focus groups to evaluate the design concept; in affinity diagramming to generate feedback about the website organisation, categories and lists; in brainstorming sessions to evaluate the screen display; and in early usability testing of the screen designs (Usability Net, 2006d).

Paper prototyping can also be used to evaluate the design and usability of the interface by using a form of think aloud protocols. Because the prototype is not interactive, you need to simulate how the prototype will behave when the participant interacts with the interface.

High-fidelity, dynamic prototypes

What is a high-fidelity prototype?

In contrast to a low-fidelity paper prototype, a high-fidelity, dynamic prototype is created using software, is computer-based, and functions similar to the final product. The high-fidelity prototype is an early working version of the final product. It resembles the final product closely by including design details and functionality, thus permitting realistic user interactions.

High-fidelity prototypes are created with software specifically designed for this purpose. Software such as Macromedia Dreamweaver and Director, Microsoft PowerPoint, Access and Visual Basic can be used to create an interactive interface.

What is the objective?

The objective of high-fidelity prototypes is to create a realistic, interactive version of the final product. These prototypes are useful for finding usability problems and to generate feedback relative to the interface design. Most often usability testing with think aloud protocols employs a high-fidelity prototype. It is useful in the later stages of the development. A high-fidelity prototype is so close to the final product that usability testing will reveal how the interface behaviour will relate to use of the final product, thus permitting strong conclusions about the usability and usefulness of the product (Lindgaard, 1994: 91).

As with low-fidelity paper prototypes, the use of high-fidelity prototypes is part of an iterative design process to develop a user-centred design. After usability testing, found issues are addressed with a revision of the interface. This process is continued until the interface meets acceptable standards.

Who are the participants?

When high-fidelity prototypes are part of a participatory design process, participants are representative stakeholders. In usability testing, the participants are usually selected from the target end-user groups. The number of participants selected will depend on the method and the stage in the development. For example, during the first round of usability testing, you might want 6–10 participants. In the second round of usability testing, when checking if design changes have addressed found issues, you might want 4–6 participants. To determine how many participants are required, see the specific descriptions of the methods.

How long will it take?

High-fidelity prototypes take longer to create than low-fidelity paper prototypes. As such, you need to allow for and invest in more time. In addition, because high-fidelity prototypes are created with special-purpose software, you need someone familiar with the software to create and revise the prototypes.

As with paper prototypes, usability methods with high-fidelity prototypes are part of an iterative design process. The length of time will vary depending on the method that you choose and the stage in the development.

What materials do you need?

You need special-purpose software such as Macromedia Dreamweaver, Microsoft PowerPoint, Microsoft Access or Visual Basic to develop an interactive prototype. Because evaluation sessions with high-fidelity prototypes are usually one-on-one, you should only need one computer with an active prototype.

As in other evaluation methods, you need all or some of the following: a script, a consent form, audio or videotaping materials, recruitment and scheduling materials, other correspondence materials and incentives. Additional materials will depend on the type of session. For the specific materials, see the descriptions of the evaluation methods.

How do you use high-fidelity prototyping?

High-fidelity prototyping generates usability feedback in the later stages of the development, when you have a clear idea of how the interface will look and function. The design of high-fidelity prototypes is best when based on information derived from previous usability design activities.

High-fidelity prototypes can be employed in usability testing methods such as think aloud protocols. The information from these sessions informs revisions to further refine the interface. For more information about think aloud protocols see the section on usability testing the website.

What are the advantages?

High-fidelity prototypes are functional, interactive prototypes that are employed in usability evaluation methods to provide feedback about how users interact with the interface so that usability decisions can be based on user needs (SAP Design Guild, 2004). High-fidelity prototypes more accurately represent the graphics, font, images and colour of the final product.

Because high-fidelity prototypes closely resemble the finished product, they are an effective marketing tool that is useful for demonstration with clients, managers or funding agents. To further illustrate the requirements document, they can be effective in conveying system behaviour and detail specifics to the development team and the developers. High-fidelity prototypes can also be valuable when developing documentation (Virzi, Sokolov and Karis, 1996: 242).

What are the disadvantages?

High-fidelity prototypes take longer to create than paper prototypes and need to be developed by someone who knows how to use special-purpose software. As such, they are more expensive to create and more difficult to revise. Because of the time invested in creating high-fidelity prototypes, usability testing might be delayed and the development team, who may be facing time pressure, might be less inclined to make changes, especially major changes, leading to an early commitment to an inferior product.

5

Usability inspection methods

Usability inspection and expert reviews are examinations of the interface, usually by experts, in order to find usability problems or issues. The objective of usability inspection, like other methods of usability evaluation, is to find 'inconsistencies, especially those that do not comply with a set of development standards' (Barnum, 2002: 35). 'Usability inspection is inexpensive, can be completed in as little as a few minutes, and can happen at any stage of design' (Brinck, Gergle and Wood, 2002: 408).

Participants are not needed to conduct usability inspections; the strength of this type of evaluation lies in the 'investigator's knowledge of how to design for usability' (Jordan, 1998: 77). The outcomes can be reported in a formal report of found issues, an informal report, or simply a presentation (Shneiderman, 1997: 127). A disadvantage of usability inspection methods is that by lacking involvement of users, there is no direct evidence related to usability problems; the process is dependent on the level of expertise of the reviewers.

Two common methods of usability inspection are heuristic evaluation and cognitive walkthroughs. Heuristic evaluations rely on usability experts to inspect the interface against a set of heuristics in order to find usability problems. In cognitive walkthroughs, experts, or occasionally non-experts, operate the website and complete real-world tasks to find usability problems. Both methods will be described in the following sections.

Heuristic evaluation

What is a heuristic evaluation?

Heuristic evaluation, a popular method of usability inspection, requires up to five expert reviewers to examine the website or page interface for usability issues taken from a list of heuristics. Heuristics can be thought of as a set of standards or principles that have been accepted by experts in the field, in this case, usability engineering. Originally developed by Nielsen and Molich (Molich and Nielsen, 1990: 338–48; Nielsen and Molich, 1990: 249–56) and later upgraded by Nielsen (1994a: 152–8), the following set of heuristics is often used as guidelines for a heuristic evaluation:

- *Visibility of system status*: The system should always keep users informed about what is going on through appropriate feedback within a reasonable time.

- *Match between system and the real world*: The system should speak the user's language, with words, phrases and concepts familiar to the user, rather than system-oriented terms. It should follow real-world conventions, making information appear in a natural and logical order.

- *User control and freedom*: Users often choose system functions by mistake and will need a clearly marked 'emergency exit' to leave the unwanted state without having to go through an extended dialogue. The system should support undo and redo.

- *Consistency and standards*: Users should not have to wonder whether different words, situations or actions mean the same thing. The system should follow platform conventions.

- *Error prevention*: Even better than good error messages is a careful design which prevents a problem from occurring in the first place. Either eliminate error-prone conditions or check for them and present users with a confirmation option before they commit to the action.

- *Recognition rather than recall*: Minimise the user's memory load by making objects, actions and options visible. The user should not have to remember information from one part of the dialogue to another. Instructions for use of the system should be visible or easily retrievable whenever appropriate.

- *Flexibility and efficiency of use*: Accelerators – unseen by the novice user – may often speed up interaction for the expert user such that the system can cater to both inexperienced and experienced users. The system should allow users to tailor frequent actions.

- *Aesthetic and minimalist design*: Dialogues should not contain information which is irrelevant or rarely needed. Every extra unit of information in a dialogue competes with the relevant units of information and diminishes their relative visibility.

- *Help users recognise, diagnose and recover from errors*: Error messages should be expressed in plain language (no codes), precisely indicate the problem, and constructively suggest a solution.

- *Help and documentation*: Even though it is better if the system can be used without documentation, it may be necessary to provide help and documentation. Any such information should be easy to search, focus on the user's task, list concrete steps to be carried out, and not be too large.

Evaluators inspect the interface several times looking for issues or problems. They might complete a set of tasks suggested by the development team or try out their own set of tasks. The report will include a list of found usability issues, the heuristic that the issue violated, the severity of the issue, and recommendations for a course of action based on sound usability principles. To indicate the severity of the issue, decide on a severity rating scale in advance. Nielsen (year unknown) recommends a severity rating scale comprised of five levels of severity:

0 = I do not agree that this is a usability problem at all.
1 = Cosmetic problem only: need not be fixed unless time is available on project.
2 = Minor usability problem: fixing this should be given low priority.
3 = Major usability problem: important to fix, so should be given high priority.
4 = Usability catastrophe: imperative to fix this before product can be released.

Heuristic evaluation can take place at any stage of the development when a prototype of the user interface is in place. The prototype can be paper mock-up, a paper prototype of the interface pages, or a computer-based working interface. Although heuristic evaluation is usually carried out when the website is capable of responding to user entries, it can be done using a series of screens on a paper prototype of the target website (Lindgaard, 1994: 122). Early in the development, heuristic evaluation can save valuable time and effort that is necessary for revisions that take place late in the development after the software has been developed.

What is the objective?

The objective of heuristic evaluation is to find usability issues and problems with the end-user interface that are not in compliance with a set of usability heuristics or generally accepted standards. The results of a heuristic evaluation are used to refine the website to make it more usable and user-centred.

Who are the participants?

Heuristic evaluation does not involve participants, only reviewers. Usually more usability problems are found if more than one reviewer inspects the website independent of the other reviewers. It is easy for reviewers, even experienced ones, to miss a usability issue, thus several reviewers produce the best results. Reviewers who are knowledgeable of both user-centred design and the subject matter of the interface are the most successful; however, even non-professionals can function as evaluators (Lindgaard, 1994: 120).

How long will it take?

Heuristic evaluation can take half a day to a week to complete depending on the type of evaluation, the website depth, the number of reviewers, and the length of the report. The actual process of the heuristic evaluation, inspecting the website or pages, varies with the size of the interface. Add additional time for a full written report and still more time if a report will include an organised summary of all reviewers' findings.

What materials do you need?

Heuristic evaluations require up to five reviewers, a prototype of the interface, a set of heuristics, a set of tasks (optional), and, for consistency among reviewers, an evaluation form. The prototype can be a mock-up, a paper prototype or a working interface. If the evaluation is early in the cycle, the prototype might be as simple as a paper prototype of the homepage. Although experts are preferred, evaluations can be performed by non-experts using the heuristics of usability standards.

Where are they held?

Provided the prototype is available, heuristic evaluations can be held anywhere. If using a functional prototype, a computer must also be available.

How do you report the results?

Summarise the data

The data from a heuristic evaluation are the found issues reported by the reviewer(s). Report each issue separately, include the heuristic on non-compliance, describe the problem, indicate the severity, include a screenshot to illustrate the problem, and include possible recommendations based on heuristic standards.

Reviewers should have their own set of found issues. Because each reviewer completes their own set of issues, data do not need to be analysed. The found issues can be reported individually and also combined in a final report.

Write the report

Each reviewer writes a report. The reports should include a description or list of the heuristics, the rating scale, the interface, the purpose of the interface, the stage of the development cycle in which the review was conducted, and the list of found usability issues.

Screenshots can be included in the report to help illustrate the problem. It is also helpful to the developers to include a full description of the problem – the circumstances that brought about the problem, a sample of the task, and the behaviour or the key strokes of the reviewer and the resulting behaviour. For consistency among reviewers, use a form to report usability problems. See Figure 5.1 for an example of such a form.

For an overall comparison, issues from all reviewers can be combined and recorded in a spreadsheet report that shows the issues on the left column and the reviewers listed across the top. The spreadsheet will list an issue and then show the responses of the reviewers.

What are the advantages?

Heuristic evaluations are quick, effective, economical, and can be conducted at any phase of the development cycle to 'uncover lots of potential usability defects' (Lindgaard, 1994: 125). They do not include users, so they are convenient and confidentiality is not an issue (Jordan, 1998: 77).

| Figure 5.1 | Example of a heuristic evaluation form to report usability problems |

Evaluator: CAG - HE – 2	Severity Rating: 2

Problem: Order inconsistency between titles in left and right windows

Evidence:

Category has subcategories, clicking on the category name shows a list of titles in the main window.

Clicking on all of the subcategories shows all of the titles in the category in the main window.

The order of the titles listed in the left clusters (in each of the subcategories) is inconsistent with the order of the titles listed in the main window.

Expectation is to have the order of titles the same in both windows.

Creates difficulty when trying to locate titles.

Explanation: Heuristics 2:

Match between system and the real world. When trying to view titles in the main window, I had trouble finding the article of interest due to inconsistency in the order between the list in the left window and the articles in the main window. This is inconsistent with expectations. The information doesn't appear in a logical order.

Possible solution and /or trade-offs:

Create consistency in the lists of titles in both windows.

Severity Rating:

0 to 4 with 0 the least severe and 4 the most severe

What are the disadvantages?

Heuristic evaluations do not provide feedback about the behaviour of users using the interface to complete real-world tasks. Results are issues of non-compliance with usability heuristics. Lindgaard (1994) describes the following disadvantages:

- several evaluations must usually be performed for maximum benefit;
- they are ideally done by experts;
- there is a high probability of 'false alarms';
- it is not always easy to distinguish between trivial and serious problems.

Jordan (1998: 78) adds that heuristic evaluations produce no direct evidence from users, so they are dependent on the expert's knowledge and experience.

Table 5.1 provides an example of how a heuristic evaluation might be conducted.

Cognitive walkthrough

What is a cognitive walkthrough?

In a cognitive walkthrough reviewers inspect the website by completing real-world tasks with a prototype of the system or the completed system (Barnum, 2002: 39). As the reviewers complete the tasks, they consider how a representative user might experience the website (Jordan, 1998: 79). They consider how easy the website is to learn and operate, what usability issues, if any, are associated with the website navigation, and whether target users have the requisite knowledge to understand and operate the website.

The prototype in a cognitive walkthrough can be as simple as a hand-drawn draft of the proposed end-user interface, or it can be a functional prototype with interactive screens. The reviewers can be expert usability professionals or members of the development team – designers, usability personnel, content experts and representative users.

| **Table 5.1** | Example – conducting a heuristic evaluation |

Identify the problem	In the later stages of the library website redesign, the development team will use a heuristic evaluation to see whether the functional prototype complies with usability standards.
Prepare materials	Develop a description of the system goals and objectives with examples of how the system will be used. Prepare a set of tasks or scenarios that evaluators can complete when inspecting the interface. Select a set of usability heuristics and severity ratings and prepare copies for all reviewers. Develop a usability form that reviewers can use to include information related to found issues (see Appendix).
Choose reviewers	Decide if you will hire reviewers to inspect the system or if you will use in-house experts, non-experts, or for university or college libraries, students who have experience or knowledge about usability. Expert reviewers will find as many as 81–90 per cent of usability issues (Danino, 2001). Evaluators who are experienced with usability standards and also with similar systems will provide the best results by finding the most usability issues. Non-experts will find about 22–29 per cent of issues (Danino, 2001).
Determine the heuristics	Decide on a set of heuristics that will be used with the evaluation and review them with the team. Also review the heuristics with the reviewers to make certain all agree on the definition. The non-experts will need more guidance and examples to understand the heuristics. Prepare a copy of the heuristics for evaluators. For example, use the heuristics originally developed by Molich and Nielsen (1990: 338–48) and later revised by Nielsen (1994a: 152–8).
Determine the rating scale	Reviewers will need to rate each issue to indicate the severity of the problem, so the development team will need to determine a rating scale. For this example, a rating scale developed by Jakob Nielsen (year unknown) is appropriate.
Complete the heuristic evaluation	The development team and the reviewers will discuss the heuristics, the rating scale and the evaluation form until all agree on the process. The reviewers will complete the inspection of the website and report found issues using the evaluation forms.

To prepare for a cognitive walkthrough, Wharton et al. (1994: 105–40) describe the following questions to consider when planning the activity:

- *Who will be the users of the system?* The reviewers need to agree on users' characteristics (e.g. their technical background) and the knowledge needed to complete the tasks. Knowledge is based on users' experience and on what they can learn from the system.

- *What tasks will be analysed?* Tasks should be realistic and represent the tasks that users will complete with the finished system.

- *What is the correct action sequence for each task?* Determine the sequence of actions necessary to complete the task.

- *How is the interface defined?* Determine how the interface will behave for each task; include a description of the prompts preceding each action and how the interface will respond.

Preparation for a cognitive walkthrough often includes a task analysis. A task analysis is the process of determining users' goals and objectives, the primary tasks that will be included in the system to enable users to accomplish their goals, and a detailed description of the steps users take in order to complete tasks (Hackos and Redish, 1998: 11–13). A task analysis describes what actions users need to take and/or the cognitive processes (mental thoughts and activities) that are necessary to complete the tasks. Understanding the task complexities and necessary completion activities will enable the reviewers to better review the interface design from the user's perspective (see the section on task analysis).

When the development team participates in the cognitive walkthrough using a paper prototype, the activity is often conducted in a group. The team is shown or given a paper prototype of the screen and asked to complete a task. To evaluate the interface from the user's perspective, reviewers consider four questions (Wharton et al., 1994: 105–40):

- Will the user try to achieve the right effect?
- Will the user notice that the correct action is available?

- Will the user associate the correct action with the effect that they are trying to achieve?

- If the correct action is performed, will the user see that progress is being made toward the solution of the task?

After the reviewers consider the task and how end-users will complete it, they discuss the task as it relates to the system design and the usability. The discussion is recorded and the found issues are noted and considered for the revision of the system.

When the cognitive walkthrough is completed with a working interface, the procedure is similar to the session with a paper prototype, except that reviewers will complete tasks as end-users might with a functional prototype.

Gaffney (2000d) describes a cognitive walkthrough employing a paper prototype and target users rather than experts as the evaluators. Participants are given a booklet with screenshots and questions about the screen display. Participants are presented with a screen displayed on an overhead projector and duplicated in the booklet and asked to imagine that they will complete a task. The group then discusses task completion. Participants are encouraged to write their thoughts in the booklet. About four tasks are completed. The notes on the discussion and the participants' notes in the booklet form the basis of the data.

What is the objective?

The objective of a cognitive walkthrough is to find usability and design issues from the user's perspective. When it is completed early in the development with a paper prototype, the results can indicate points in the system that might be confusing to a target user, navigation that is unclear, and terminology that is unfamiliar. In the early stages, found issues are more easily and inexpensively addressed.

When used late in the development with a working prototype of the proposed website, the results of the cognitive walkthrough can indicate usability problems associated with the interaction of the target user with the proposed website.

Who are the participants?

A facilitator, often accompanied by a note-taker, leads the activity. The participants in a cognitive walkthrough often include only the development team as the reviewers – the developers, designers, usability personnel and content experts. Some cognitive walkthroughs include target end-users as the participants and the reviewers.

How long will it take?

A cognitive walkthrough discussion can take one to two hours to complete. Assuming that the task analysis and user needs requirements have already been completed, the preparation for the cognitive walkthrough can take from six to 24 hours. Analysis of the data and completion of the report with recommendations can take two to three days.

What materials do you need?

You can complete a simple cognitive walkthrough with a low-fidelity or high-fidelity prototype of the system. In the early stages of development, cognitive walkthroughs can be completed using a hand-drawn paper prototype or a more sophisticated application-based paper prototype. The prototypes can be prepared as single pages or in a booklet of screen displays that include questions and prompts. You need a set for each participant, the facilitator and the note-taker. In the later stages of the development process, a working prototype can be used. You need the functional prototype and a computer for reviewers.

What are the advantages?

The cognitive walkthrough is cost-effective and takes little time to produce results regarding the usability of the system (Jordan, 1998: 80). The method can be used at any stage of the development process although it is most valuable when used in the early stages of design. The evaluation method can be used with both low-fidelity (paper) and high-fidelity (working interface) prototypes.

What are the disadvantages?

The cognitive walkthrough, a non-empirical method, usually does not involve end-users interacting with the system. As such, the reviewers will not be able to observe or measure the users' behaviour with the website. The evaluation results are based on the reviewers' knowledge of usability and their knowledge of cognitive processes, thus enabling them to anticipate users' behaviour (Jordan, 1998: 80; Barnum, 2002: 40).

6

Usability testing the website

Usability testing is a method of measuring the usability of a website by observing typical end-users using the site to complete real-world tasks. The facilitator notes problems or issues. Tasks, usually designed by the development team, are part of task scenarios, descriptions of typical situations that users encounter when operating the website. Often usability testing includes think aloud protocols, that is, participants are asked to think out loud while completing the tasks.

'The goal of a usability test is to find the product's weaknesses and problems so that you can improve the product before it goes out to users' (Dumas and Redish, 1999: 193). You need to determine whether the website is user-centred and usable, whether the website is easy to use, and whether users are able to complete the tasks for which the system was designed. Based on your results, you can refine the interface toward creating a user-centred design.

Conduct usability testing in order to inform the design of a new product, to improve an existing product, to compare two or more products that your library is considering purchasing, or to evaluate a finished product (Jordan, 1998: 81–2). Usability testing is most effective when it is used iteratively throughout the development from the earlier stages of the design with a product prototype to the final product using a functioning website. Each testing cycle is followed by a redesign of the website interface until the interface meets accepted usability standards.

Although it might be tempting to conduct a focus group in order to generate usability information, focus groups, as well many other usability methods, will not produce information about how users interact with the website. Quite simply, as Krug (2000: 140) notes, 'focus groups are not usability tests'. He goes on to explain that focus groups 'are not good for learning about whether your website interface is usable and how to improve it' (Krug, 2000: 141). Usability testing, during which you observe participants complete tasks and talk about their experiences, produces information about the website's usability, helps you detect problems, and provides hints about how to fix problems. Krug (2000: 141–3) describes several important aspects of usability testing:

- To find out if your website really works, you have to test. 'Testing reminds you that not everyone thinks the way you do, knows what you know, uses the web the way you do.'

- Testing always shows you how to improve the website, even when testing with only one user.

- A simple usability test earlier in the development cycle is better than a more sophisticated test late in the cycle.

- Results of usability testing, when taken with your experience, judgment and common sense, will help you to make better decisions about the design of the website.

- Usability testing is part of an iterative design cycle of testing, fixing and retesting until the design meets usability standards.

Planning and preparation

'Planning for usability testing is critical to a successful test' (Dumas and Redish, 1999: 105–7). To plan effectively, consider what aspects of the product might not be easy to use and what task scenarios will test those aspects. When recruiting participants, consider who will represent the target end-user groups and how you will screen volunteers to select those who meet the criteria. Before beginning the testing sessions you need to make some decisions about the evaluation:

- determine the objectives of the usability test – what will be tested;
- write the task scenarios and tasks;
- determine what participant behaviour you will focus on when observing task completion;
- determine what quantitative data you will collect during task completion;
- determine the methods of analysing and interpreting the data.

Task scenario

What is a task scenario?

Task scenarios 'are descriptive stories about the intended use of the product' (Booth, 1989: 117). They describe a realistic situation that end-users might encounter, and task(s) that end-users might want to accomplish when using the website. Rather than simply a list of tasks, scenarios are descriptions of typical situations. Every scenario includes at least one typical task and often multiple tasks.

Before beginning the design of task scenarios, you need to determine the scope of the testing. The scope defines the regions of the website that will be tested. Because many websites are too broad to test every element of the website, you need to determine the most critical elements of the website. Task scenarios focus on the most important and typical functionality and tasks. A task analysis can provide information that will help you to understand and prioritise tasks (see the section on task analysis).

Consider the critical functionality of the website – what participants need to be able to do in order to complete the most basic tasks. Test the elements of the website that you expect will have a high frequency of use or will satisfy a basic need of end-users as they interact with the system. Test the primary website navigation and the page navigation links because participants need to be able to move through the website without getting lost or frustrated.

Design task scenarios as questions that are 'targeted and specific' (Brinck, Gergle and Wood, 2002: 426). If the website is very broad, and you still need to test the entire website, you might consider breaking down the testing into two parts. One set of participants will complete the first group of scenarios and the second set of participants will complete the second group.

How do I create task scenarios

When you design task scenarios, consider the main objectives of the website and the scope of your evaluation. Create a list of your test objectives and use it as a guide to the subsequent activities. Then relate the tasks and scenarios to the objectives. Nielsen (1993: 185) suggests that 'the tasks need to be small enough to be completed within the time limits of the usability test, but they should not be so small that they become trivial'. For example, if an objective of the library website is to provide easy access to scholarly resources found in databases, then you need to create a scenario that describes a situation when users need to find resources by searching scholarly databases.

Try to have at least one scenario for each primary objective. The task scenario should help you answer the questions you have about the website's usability. When creating task scenarios, consider the following (Barnum, 2002: 199; Dumas and Redish, 1999: 172–82; Rosson and Carroll, 2001: 17–19; Torres, 2002: 231).

Short and clearly stated

Keep the scenarios short, clearly stated, and unambiguous. Include in the task sheet the objective of the scenario, the written description of the scenarios, a description of the setting or starting state, the tasks and the desired actions of the participants. Include the actions that will indicate success of the tasks (see Figure 6.1).

Figure 6.1 Example of a task scenario for a library website usability test

Objective: Participants can find the special online collections search page, a specific collection listed on the page, and return to the homepage.

Scenario: You are a computer science student and are researching the early work of Herbert A. Simon. The library website has full-text collections of archival materials. Some highlight the achievements of notable individuals.

Task 1: Find the Herbert A. Simon Collection.
Task 2: Return to the homepage.

Desired action: Full-Text Collections → Archives → Simon Collection → Access → Search the Collection → Home (alternatives accepted)

Criteria for success:
Task 1: Participants will find the Simon Collection search page.
Task 2: Participants will return to the website homepage.

Include enough information

Include enough information in scenarios so that all participants can complete the task. Remember that task scenarios will be used with all participants regardless of their knowledge, background or discipline. Shown in Figure 6.2 is a task scenario for usability testing of an information retrieval system (search engine) available on a library website.

Because all participants will complete this task and many will be outside the engineering discipline, we noted that the article was in the engineering subject area, something that requires special knowledge of the subject area that not all participants might have. We provided some information but not all for the citation. This is a typical task that students might need to complete.

Figure 6.2	Example of a task scenario that includes enough information for participants to complete the tasks

Objective: Using part of a citation to an article, participants will find the article citation and the full-text of the article. Participants will use subject sets and enter the search query correctly. They will recognise and use the SFX icon correctly.

Scenario: Imagine that you are writing a paper for your engineering class. A friend gave you a partial citation for a relevant article which you would like to find.

You know that the article is titled "The March of the Robot Dogs" and is written by Robert Sparrow. It is in the journal *Ethics and Information Technology*.

Task 2: Find the article citation.

Task 2: Go to the full text of the article.

Desired action: Select the Engineering subject → enter the author's name in the search query box, Sparrow, Robert → find the citation → click on SFX to find the full article (alternatives accepted)

Criteria for success: Select the Engineering subject set; enter the search query; find the citation for "The March of the Robot Dogs"; find the full text of the article.

Figure 6.3 Examples of general and specific wording for task scenarios

Scenario A – (recommended) is general and does not use the website interface language:

Imagine that you have checked out a few books, and you're not sure when they are due. Check your library account to find out when your books are due. Return to the homepage.

Scenario B – (not recommended) is too specific and uses the website interface language:

Imagine that you have checked out a number of books, and you're not sure when they are due. Go to "User Self Services" and check your user account to see when the books are due. Return to the homepage.

Write in the users' language

Avoid using the language of the website interface or the names of the specific navigational links participants will use when completing the tasks. When you use the language of the website interface, you cannot determine whether the participants understand the terminology. For example, consider the different wording used with the same task shown in Figure 6.3.

Create a short story

Avoid writing scenarios as a set of instructions or a list of steps; create a short story that describes a realistic, typical situation and task. Include at least one goal and possibly additional subgoals. Consider the example of a scenario for usability testing of a library website shown in Figure 6.4.

Select the most significant tasks

Although the website will support a great many tasks, from the very basic to advanced, you will not be able to include all of them. You need to select 5–10 of the most significant

Figure 6.4	Examples of task scenarios for usability testing of a library website

Scenario A (recommended) is written like a story that describes a situation and tasks:

The Libraries' website has full-text collections of archival materials. Some highlight the achievements of notable individuals. Find the Herbert A. Simon Collection search page. Return to the homepage.

Scenario B (not recommended) is written like a set of steps or instructions:

On the homepage, click on <Full-Text Collections>

On the <Full-Text Collections> page click on <Archives>

On the Archives page click on <Simon Collection>

On the Simon Collection Search Page click on <Home>

tasks to represent the typical tasks end-users will attempt to complete. The tasks you choose will be consistent with the objectives of the testing. Include easy tasks as well as harder tasks.

Arrange scenarios in a logical order

Arrange task scenarios in the sequence that they will most likely be used in practice (Rubin, 1994: 179–83). This helps to keep the tasks authentic and consistent with how people might learn how to use the website in practice. For a library website, you will probably have about ten scenarios. Try to begin with an easier task that most participants will be able to complete and end with a task that will leave participants with a feeling of accomplishment (Nielsen, 1993: 186). Each scenario might have multiple parts that relate to the main scenario. Try to limit the number and difficulty of tasks to what can be accomplished within an hour. You can determine the length of time by trying them out yourself and by timing task completion during the pilot test.

Post-test questionnaires

What is a post-test questionnaire?

A post-test questionnaire often follows usability testing and provides a method of collecting additional evaluation information about the website's strengths and weaknesses. Most importantly, the wording in questions and statements in post-test questionnaires should be neutral and not lead participants to a specific response (Barnum, 2002: 202–3). (See Chapter 3 for guidelines on the design of questionnaires).

Post-test questionnaires include specific questions about the website interface. They can be used to collect information about the ease of use of the website interface, the clarity of the language, or the participant's opinions about a specific task. Dumas and Redish (1999: 208–12) suggest the following reasons for using a written questionnaire:

- to compare opinions by asking every participant the same question;
- so that you do not forget to ask the question.

A post-test questionnaire often includes both quantitative (e.g. rating scale) and qualitative (e.g. essay-type) items that take a more general view of the product. They include items that could refer to any product and those that refer to the specific product in usability testing. Participants are often eager to please, so their responses might be overly positive as compared with their behaviour on the tasks (Barnum, 2002: 238). However, the questionnaire responses do provide a basis for comparison among items to gauge the product elements that are most in need of refinement or attention.

Figure 6.5 Example of items that can be used for a rating scale in a post-test questionnaire

		1	2	3	4	5		NA
It was easy to learn this system.	Strongly disagree	☐	☐	☐	☐	☐	Strongly agree	☐
The system gives me error messages that clearly tell me how to fix the problem.	Strongly disagree	☐	☐	☐	☐	☐	Strongly agree	☐
It is easy to find the information I need.	Strongly disagree	☐	☐	☐	☐	☐	Strongly agree	☐
The screen instructions are easy to understand.	Strongly disagree	☐	☐	☐	☐	☐	Strongly agree	☐
The names of links and labels are easy to understand.	Strongly disagree	☐	☐	☐	☐	☐	Strongly agree	☐

How do I create a post-test questionnaire?

Rating scales (e.g. Likert scale) are often used to gauge participants' subjective reactions, attitudes and perceptions about website usability. Questionnaires provide participants with an opportunity to register their feelings on many aspects of the product that are consistent with a usable product. Consider the portion of a post-test questionnaire shown in Figure 6.5 which includes examples of items that can be included in a rating scale following think aloud protocols. In addition to the ratings, include an option for participants to indicate that the item is 'not applicable' (NA) to their experience.

Although rating scales are common, it is not unusual to add a few open-ended essay type items following the rating scale. Although essay-type questions are more difficult and time-consuming to analyse, they result in a broader range of

| Figure 6.6 | Examples of essay-type items used in a post-test questionnaire |

Please use the space below each item (or use the back of this paper) to indicate how you feel about the website.

What did you like the most about the website?

What did you like the least about the website?

What suggestions do you have to improve the website?

Please add additional comments.

responses that often gives clues or suggestions about how to improve the product's functionality and usability. Consider the essay-type items shown in Figure 6.6 for inclusion in a post-test questionnaire. Leave additional space for the responses.

Like all other usability evaluation methods, conduct pilot testing of the post-test questionnaire to find problems, provide ideas for other questions, determine which questions are confusing, and get an idea of how long it will take to complete (Rubin, 1994: 205–6). Refine the questionnaire based on pilot testing.

Tips on conducting usability testing

Consider the following tips when planning, developing and conducting usability testing (Rubin, 1994: 92–5; Dumas and Redish, 1999: 291–304).

Stay organised

Keep materials (e.g. blank and completed forms, notes and audiotapes) together in a labelled file folder. Label all materials with the project name, the participant's identifying information and the date. Use checklists.

Be consistent

Treat all participants the same and use scripts to make certain each session proceeds in the same manner as previous sessions. Have the same person conduct all sessions. Have specific goals in mind that were determined before the tests were developed.

Conduct pilot testing

Pilot testing will help you to refine your testing with respect to the difficulty of tasks, clarity of vocabulary and test items, and other problems.

Keep daily records

Keep a running list of found problems and issues by summarising your notes immediately after the sessions. Determine in advance what quantitative data to collect (e.g. task completion time, error number) and create forms to record the data. Focus on the participant and their actions and verbalisations during the testing.

Recruit enough representative participants

For formal usability testing, usually eight to ten participants drawn from typical user groups (e.g. experienced and novice users and various disciplines) will provide great feedback.

However, for informal or follow-up testing, four to five participants will be enough to provide good feedback, to test the revisions, and to find most errors.

Keep interactions to a minimum

Keep interruptions during testing to a minimum in order to avoid influencing the participant. Let participants complete their tasks at their own pace. Encourage them to think out loud. Use neutral words when asking questions.

Decide when the task is complete

The participant needs to indicate when the task is complete. Avoid announcing that the task is complete until the participant is ready. If they tend to spend additional time during testing, they might also do this at their home or office, so allow them to do so. These additional steps need to be documented.

One exception is when the participant says the task is complete when it is not. In this situation, if the participant is not too frustrated or you have seen enough, encourage the participant to continue.

Always consider the participant

In all situations be compassionate and consider the participant first. Be consistent in your treatment of all participants. Always remember that you are testing the product, not the user of the product, so never blame the participant.

Think aloud protocols

When people refer to usability testing, they are often referring to think aloud protocols. Nielsen, a recognised expert in the field of usability testing, describes the importance of think aloud protocols by saying, 'Thinking aloud may be the single most valuable usability engineering method' (Nielsen, 1993: 195). During think aloud protocols participants are observed and recorded as they complete real-world tasks using a prototype of the proposed website or the actual website. During task completion the participants are encouraged to talk about their thoughts, feelings and opinions about the website. 'While verbalizing their thoughts, the test users reveal their view of the computer system, and this lets us identify their major misconceptions' (Nielsen, 1993: 195).

The process of observing and recording participants as they verbalise their thoughts during an activity stems from the early work on human cognition and information processing of K. Anders Ericsson and Herbert A. Simon (for more on verbal reports, see Ericsson and Simon, 1984, 1993). Ericsson and Simon (1993) found a close connection between thinking and verbal reports by observing participants verbalise their thoughts while completing tasks. Observing participants as they complete tasks limits errors caused by participant reports that rely on long-term memory. The method of verbal reports has increasingly been used with the evaluation of computer applications and the interaction of users.

Nielsen (2001b) argues that 'users' self-reported data is typically three steps removed from the truth', and reminds us of the three basic rules of usability:

- watch what people actually do;

- do not believe what people say they do;

- definitely do not believe what people predict they may do in the future.

He goes on to say that people tend to modify what they actually think to meet more closely what they think you want to hear. People are really telling you what they remember doing, not necessarily what they actually did. Thus he recommends observing people as they complete tasks to learn more about the usability of a system.

Think aloud protocols are a method of empirically evaluating the interface. Empirical testing methods use observations and measurements to yield quantitative data about the evaluation. In the case of think aloud protocols, examples of quantitative data include task completion time, task completion rates, and error rates. The value of quantitative measurement in evaluation is that it provides benchmark as well as comparison data. During iterative design, quantitative measurement indicates the extent to which problems have been addressed. The results of think aloud protocols yield a list of usability problems as well as a method of prioritising them (Nielsen, 1993: 18).

The session can be video or audio-recorded. Think aloud protocols can be used with a paper prototype of the website interface, a functional computer-based prototype, or the actual website when it has been designed and developed. To reduce costs Nielsen (1994b) recommends taking usability testing out of the lab, eliminating videotaping and using fewer participants. Think aloud protocols can be used at any stage of the development cycle, although they are often used with a functioning website towards the later stages of the development cycle.

What is the objective?

At any stage in the development, the primary objective of think aloud protocols is to find usability problems or issues with the target website and to learn from users why they are having problems in order to redesign the website to make it more user-centred. Booth (1989: 118) describes problems and issues as a 'usability defect', which he defines as 'anything in the product which prevents a target user completing a target task with reasonable effort and within a reasonable time'. He suggests that by finding usability defects we can focus on the issues that cause problems and address the issues to further refine the product.

In the early stages when the best draft of a website is a paper prototype, the main objective is to find problems with the design and primary navigation before coding. In the later stages of the design when a functional prototype is available, the primary objective is to evaluate the interaction of users with the website to learn more about the usability issues in order to refine the website.

The facilitator's observations of the participants' behaviour and the recordings of their verbalisations as they complete the tasks provide information that is used to determine problems, issues or attitudes related to the website interface. The transcription of the verbalisations provides a mental model of the participants' motivating behaviour as they complete tasks. The verbalisations also indicate why mistakes are made and how to redesign the interface to address the problems. The results of think aloud protocols are used to further refine the interface and to improve the usability.

What is the role of the facilitator or other team members?

The test team can include a member of the development team and the usability specialist along with a note-taker. A member of the development team can be present to observe first-hand the problems that participants encounter while interacting with the website. This information will make it easier for the usability specialist to convince developers of the need to address found issues. The note-taker serves as an additional observer of participants' behaviour and verbalisations, increasing the amount of information that is collected and thus the credibility of the study.

However, usability testing is often conducted by the human factors researcher or usability specialists alone who will act as the facilitator and the note-taker. Human factors researchers are the likely persons to conduct the testing because they are familiar with experimental methodology and the basics of usability engineering related to usable products (Rubin, 1994: 65–7). Lacking usability specialists on the team, others who can conduct the testing include training specialists, team members or external consultants.

Facilitators create a non-threatening atmosphere by making the participants feel welcome. They consider participants' self-esteem and do not let them get too frustrated, are sympathetic when participants have problems, and graciously thank them when the session is completed (Krug, 2000: 155). Facilitators introduce the session, and guide participants through the task scenarios, always treating them respectfully. They offer refreshments, explain the objective of the session and the role of the participants, and they explain the concept of informed consent (Dumas and Redish, 1999: 274–86; Barnum, 2002: 210–13).

An important responsibility of facilitators is to explain the process of thinking out loud and, during the sessions, to remind participants to think out loud. 'In presenting the process to the user, the facilitator should emphasize that the team is very interested in understanding what the user is *thinking about* when performing the task, not just the user's description of the task itself' (Dumas and Redish, 1999: 274–86; Barnum, 2002: 235). When participants get caught up in completing the tasks, they often forget to think out loud. Facilitators can prompt participants by asking questions such as the following:

- Can you tell me what you're thinking about now?

- I see that you're scanning. What were you looking for on the page?

- Can you tell me why you chose that last action?

Facilitators remain neutral during the sessions and observe what participants do and say, although they do not comment on participants' behaviour or suggest methods for completing the tasks. This is sometimes difficult if you usually teach when interacting with students. However, teaching or showing participants how to use the website during the testing interrupts the session and destroys the simulation of working without help. To avoid affecting the outcome, try to reserve answers to questions or opportunities for teaching for the end of the session.

Facilitators take notes, time the activity, and try not to offer help until the participant is frustrated and gives up on the task; 'the experimenter should not let a user struggle endlessly with a task if the user is clearly bogged down and getting desperate' (Nielsen, 1993: 182). If the task must be ended before the participant successfully completes it, the facilitator records the task failure and then provides a hint so that the task can be completed, and the participant can move on to the next task. By allowing the participant to proceed, there is no data loss due to failure to complete one part of a task. Facilitators end the session by thanking participants for their time and input and offering them the incentive.

Who are the participants?

When selecting participants, the important point to remember is that you are not recruiting so that you can generalise to a larger group, as in a research study; rather, you are recruiting participants who will provide you with the most useful information about problems and issues with the target website (Dumas and Redish, 1999: 127). To gain the most useful feedback, select participants to represent the target population of users and who are diverse with respect to computer expertise, domain expertise, age, gender, discipline, and familiarity with the target website or type of software. Choosing a representative group of participants as well as representative tasks is important to increase the validity of the study (Dumas and Redish, 1999: 169).

The number of participants varies from three to ten, depending on the stage in the development cycle and the type of evaluation (formal or informal), the amount of time available, the need for representation and the project's budget. Based on empirical studies, Nielsen and researcher Tom Landauer determined that, 'The maximum benefit-cost ratio is achieved when using between three and five subjects' (Nielsen, 1994b). The number of found errors increases with the number of participants, although decreases after eight participants. Nielsen recommends using fewer participants for each session and then repeated use of think aloud protocol testing following an iterative design process of design, test and redesign cycles.

How long will it take?

The entire process of usability testing from the design of the evaluation to the completion of the report can take from three to 12 weeks depending on the objective of the sessions (overall usability testing or retesting after revisions), the number of tasks, the recruiting process, the number of participants, and the method of communicating the results.

When conducting think aloud protocols as formal usability testing of a completed, functional website, the evaluation might include eight to ten participants, and the sessions would probably be audio or videotaped. Planning and recruiting, conducting the sessions, transcribing the tapes, analysing and interpreting the data, and communicating the findings in a formal report can take as long as six to 12 weeks for the entire process.

For formal usability testing, allow about one to two hours for each session of think aloud protocols. This will provide enough time to welcome participants and present instructions, complete the task scenarios, the final review, and post-test questionnaire (optional). The length of time will vary depending on the number of tasks and the amount of participant verbalisations.

When think aloud protocols are carried out in the early stages of the development cycle with a paper prototype, the sessions can be shorter, and the results can be a list of findings in a quick report to the team. When used as a follow-up to formal usability testing, the activity might involve fewer participants than the formal testing, and the findings can be communicated in a quick report. These types of evaluations can be completed within three weeks.

Dumas and Redish (1999: 103–5) suggest ways in which usability testing can be shortened to less than four weeks:

- use in-house usability specialists who know the procedures and facilities for such testing;
- test only a few features of the product;
- select participants from a previously established pool of people who meet the criteria;
- write a short report.

What materials do you need?

You need all or some of the following: recruitment and scheduling materials, a method of screening volunteers, other correspondence materials, consent form, and beverages and incentives. You need to complete a task analysis in order to design task scenarios and a series of tasks (see the sections on task analysis and task scenarios) and a post-test questionnaire. Other options include an experienced facilitator, a note-taker, and video and/or audiotaping materials.

Where are they held?

They are held in a lab or in a private, quiet place, for example, an office where participants will not be disturbed while they interact with the interface and talk. The space should be large enough for the participant to work at the computer, while the facilitator observes and guides the activity, and a note-taker observes the activity.

How do you pilot test think aloud protocols?

As with other usability evaluation methods, conduct pilot testing before you begin the testing sessions. Pilot test your procedure, tasks and scenarios, recruitment materials and post-test questionnaire. Use all materials as you would in the actual usability testing situation.

Pilot testing affords the opportunity to time the tasks and the session, enabling you to revise testing if tasks are too long or too complex. It helps to determine if the materials and/or equipment (e.g. audio and video-recorders) and software are operating smoothly and as expected; if the scenarios are written clearly, are reasonable with respect to completion time and users' ability, and produce relevant data; and if the post-test questionnaire items are clear to users and yield relevant information (Nielsen, 1993: 174–5). Use feedback from pilot testing to refine instructions, questionnaires, test tasks and scenarios, clarify definitions, and reveal inconsistencies (Nielsen, 1993: 174–5).

Two methods can be used to try out your plans for the think aloud protocols – a walkthrough by the development team members and an actual pilot test with target users (Barnum, 2002: 217–20). During a walkthrough, members examine the script, try out scenarios with the prototype, review the recruitment materials, and examine any other resources or equipment that will be used during the testing. The team provides feedback leading to revisions as needed.

A pilot test using the revised materials and equipment is then conducted with one to three target users. Because this is a trial run of the actual think aloud protocols, it is important to follow all procedures as you would with the actual testing. If no problems are found, the results of the pilot testing can be used as part of the actual testing.

Otherwise, address found problems and use the revised materials and procedures in usability testing.

How do you communicate the results?

Plan what data to collect

First determine what data to collect. Think aloud protocols enable you to collect both empirical (quantitative) and non-empirical (qualitative) data. While empirical data can be used to measure the severity of the problem, help you to prioritise the issues and provide benchmarks in iterative design, non-empirical data can be used to find methods of addressing the problems. The following subsections provide examples of data collected during think aloud protocols (Booth, 1989: 120–4; Rubin, 1994: 259–64; Jordan, 1998: 18–23; Dumas and Redish, 1999: 310–11).

Notes of your observations

Notes of your observations as participants complete the tasks are indicators of behaviour. Your notes can capture behaviour that may not be otherwise evident, especially if you are not video-recording the sessions. For example, you can note if a participant looks frustrated after many attempts on a task, or based on your observations of the cursor movement, whether the user explored the entire page before selecting a link.

Summarise your notes for each task and look for indicators of usability problems or issues relevant to task completion. Look out for similar behaviour among participants. For example, you might note that participants become frustrated when they are unable to return to the homepage after completing their first task.

Transcripts of the verbalisations

Transcripts of participants' verbalisations are useful indicators of their mental process. When a user makes an unlikely choice to achieve a result, you might wonder why. Their verbalisations are indicators of what they were thinking. Understanding the mental process is helpful when deciding how to address the found issues.

For example, during usability testing of a federated search product, the participants all failed to log in, even though the developers provided numerous indicators on the homepage. Participants' responses, shown in Figure 6.7, indicate why the page indicators failed (George, 2006: 6). Quotes from participants about found usability issues are also helpful to further illustrate the problem to the development team.

Figure 6.7   **Excerpt from a usability report showing use of participants' verbalisations**

All participants, completely unaware that they had to log in, failed to log in. When asked to complete a search, they began with the Basic Search in the locked position using the default subject search, Library Catalogues – inappropriate for article searching.

Though some commented that they noticed the padlock icon (used to indicate a locked resource and also used as a link to the log in page), they did not recognise it as an indication to log in.

> "It just looked like some sort of symbol. I've seen a lock before but it's down in the right had corner and it tells you that the place is secure to type in your credit card number." [P7]

Instructions on the Basic Search page, written in normal text size, clearly state that users must log in, however, only one participant noticed them, and only after experiencing problems:

> "I didn't read that at all. Now that we've finished two tasks, I just now see the 'log in log out click the padlock,' but only after I've been using this for 15 minutes." [P8]

Another indicated her frustration and a possible solution,

> "I would rather have a main log in before you even attempt to look at your topics or try to do your tasks." [P7]

Interspersed throughout the formal report, quotes add credibility to the findings.

Task error rate

Task error rate is a measure of errors for each task. 'The errors that occur at user interfaces are potentially one of the most useful sources of information' (Booth, 1989: 121). Errors indicate where problems exist and to some degree the extent or severity of the error. This information is useful to gauge whether the product is effective and efficient for the specific task. To calculate the error rate you first need to determine the number of errors for each task.

Errors occur during usability evaluation when the result of an action is not what the participant intended. Errors or usability defects can be described as 'anything in the product which prevents a target user achieving a target task with reasonable effort and within a reasonable time' (Booth, 1989: 128). When using a library website, for example, the participant may hit a navigational link that goes to an unexpected page and then need to go back and try a different link. This action is considered an error. Reasonable effort and reasonable time need to be defined in advance of the testing.

Errors are not all equal in severity. Jordan (1998: 20–2) describes three levels of errors – minor error, major error, and catastrophic or fatal error:

- *Minor error* is one which the user corrects almost immediately and causes little problem for the participant. They are mildly annoying. An example of a minor error is when the user enters an author's name in a search box using an incorrect format, but notices the error before completing the search.

- *Major error* is one which the participant recognises and corrects, but the time involved is more than in the minor error. Adapting the above example, the participant enters an author's name using an incorrect format in a search box and completes several searches before recognising and correcting the error.

- *Catastrophic or fatal error* is one which prevents the participant from completing the task. Using the same example, the participant enters an author's name using an incorrect format in a search box, completes several searches, and then gives up on the author search, leading to task failure.

The task error rate is the measure of the number of errors that all participants had while completing a task. It is calculated for each task using the formula:

(total number of errors / total number of attempts) × 100

The task error rate can be used to help prioritise problems. A higher error rate as compared with error rates of other tasks indicates a more difficult task. Consider also the severity of the error. A minor error is less important than a catastrophic error. The error rate and severity can be used as a benchmark in an iterative design process. When the task is tested again after the redesign, a lower error rate and severity for the task indicate that the problem was addressed successfully.

Task completion rate

Task completion rate is the measure of the number of successful completions for each task. A task completion rate is calculated for each task using the formula:

$$(\text{number of successful completions / total number of attempts}) \times 100$$

The task completion rate, a measure of the difficulty level of the task, can be used to help prioritise problems. A higher completion rate as compared with rates of other tasks indicates an easier task. It also can be used as a benchmark in an iterative design process. When the task is tested again after the redesign, a higher completion rate for the task indicates that the problem was addressed successfully.

Task completion time

Task completion time is the amount of time it takes a participant to complete the task. A task completion time is recorded each time a task is completed either successfully or unsuccessfully. The average of the task completion time for all attempts is the measure of the completion time.

It is also helpful to note the extremes – the most and least time needed. Noting which user group was represented for the extreme completion time can be helpful when prioritising the task and planning the revisions. For example, novice users tend to need the most time to complete a task. If the product is used frequently, then novice users can be expected to improve.

Completion time is useful as a benchmark in an iterative design process. When the task is retested with different representative users after the redesign, lower rates of time indicate that the problems were addressed successfully. It is also useful as a measure of efficiency, although consider the complexity of the task along with the completion time. A more complicated task will normally take longer to complete than an easy task.

Post-test questionnaire

Post-test questionnaire responses from all participants are averaged for each question or statement. If the questionnaire is short, say about ten items, use the results carefully. It is not unusual for participants to respond in a positive manner even though they had trouble completing tasks. Participants might be influenced by a desire to please the facilitator. The responses are helpful to prioritise issues when comparing items. They can be summarised in a table or illustrated chart and be included as part of the formal report or located in the appendices.

Post-test questionnaire suggestions and comments frequently follow a questionnaire or rating scale. When summarised, they can help you to address the problem issues during the redesign.

Compile the data

After all think aloud protocol sessions have been completed, you need to compile the data. 'Type up your notes soon after testing to make sure you don't forget anything' (Brinck et al., 2002: 439). This can be an ongoing process that is done after each testing session. Compile the data by summarising the results from all participants for each task.

The quantitative data can be analysed by describing the data (e.g. the task error rate or the task completion rate) for each task. Summarise the data by reporting the average and the range (the highest and lowest score) of the ratings (Dumas and Redish, 1999: 318). The summary of the task completion rate, in addition to other quantitative data, can be reported in a table (see Figure 6.8).

The qualitative data, the transcripts of the verbalisations and your observations can be grouped and summarised for

Figure 6.8 Table to report quantitative data (e.g. task completion rate) in think aloud protocols

Task scenario

Imagine that you're taking a psychology class, and you need additional information about Sigmund Freud for a presentation. Show me a full-text article about Sigmund Freud. Show me how you would e-mail the reference to yourself. Examine the list of found resources and select a second resource about Freud.

Tasks	Successful completion	
	no.	rate
1a. Find a full text article on Sigmund Freud. (8 attempts)	4	50%
1b. E-mail the reference. (7 attempts)	6	86%
1c. Select a second resource. (7 attempts)	5	71%

each task. The suggestions or comments can be summarised by content and subject. For example, include all comments about the screen display together. Do the same for other similar comments. Assign IDs to participants (e.g. P1–P5) to avoid using their names. Include quotations from participants that further illustrate any problems or issues that you describe (see Figure 6.9).

Based on the quantitative and qualitative data that you recorded, you can determine the severity of the problems. Consider the severity ratings based on the number of people who experienced the problem, how the problem impacts the

Figure 6.9 Example use of participants' quotations to help illustrate a point in the usability test report

Issue 2:   Browser *back* button
Severity: Medium

Participants who used the browser back button to navigate had problems returning to previously viewed pages.

"The back here [pointing to the browser back button], when you try to go back to the search, requires a little fighting before you get to go there." [P2]

completion of the task, and how frequently the problem might occur during typical use (Nielsen, year unknown). To indicate the severity of the issue, decide on a severity rating scale in advance.

Interpret the results

When the data are compiled, interpret the results for each task, determine the severity level of problems, and make recommendations about how to address the problems. When you make recommendations, consider the severity of the problem and the difficulty and time requirements for developers to address the problem.

If you have conducted formal think aloud protocols, you can report the results in a formal report. The report communicates the findings to the development team and other interested stakeholders and provides a record for future examination. You can also report the results in an oral presentation (see the section on writing reports).

When using think aloud protocols in the second round of testing to check changes made after formal think aloud protocols, or when they are used early in the design process with early prototypes, an informal quick report can be effective to present results quickly. The quick report can be presented orally to the development team. Quick reports take little time to complete and enable the team to continue promptly to the next step.

What are the advantages?

The primary advantage of think aloud protocols is that they provide an opportunity to observe how representative users interact with the system and complete real-world tasks. They enable the facilitator to detect problems and issues with the interface. In addition, the verbalisations of the participants help the facilitator to learn the cause of the problems, which can provide insight when redesigning the interface and improving usability. 'Participants' verbalisations make it possible to understand not only what problems they have with an interface, but also *why* these problems arise ... They can lead directly to design solutions' (Jordan, 1998: 58).

Think aloud protocol sessions, because they follow a consistent design structure, can also be used to obtain objective, quantitative data such as task completion rates, completion time and error numbers. In addition, think aloud protocols generate a lot of information with few participants.

What are the disadvantages?

The act of verbalising thoughts might cause interference with the actual act of completing tasks; participants might want to rationalise their actions to the moderator (Jordan, 1998: 58–9). Verbalising might also increase the actual time the participant needs to complete a task. In addition, coding and analysis are difficult and time-consuming, and the value of the sessions is dependent on the analyst's skill and knowledge (Lindgaard, 1994: 114). Despite best efforts, usability testing results have some limitations: testing (even field testing) is an artificial situation; test results do not prove that a product works; and participants are seldom fully representative of the target population (Rubin, 1994: 27). Tables 6.1 and 6.2 provide examples of how one might plan and facilitate a think aloud session.

Table 6.1	Example – planning for a think aloud protocol
Identify the problem	We were in the later stages of the redesign of the library website. We were interested in finding usability problems and methods of addressing the problems.
Prepare materials	The materials for usability testing included: • recruitment materials: a recruitment e-mail to post on bulletin boards or e-mail to potential participants, a demographic screening survey designed with web-based survey software, and a scheduling e-mail; • a task analysis, task scenarios, and script; • reminder e-mail, thank you e-mail, a consent form, and a participant form for recording additional demographic information; • task sheets that list task scenarios and tasks, note-taking materials; • audio-recorder and one tape for each participant including extra batteries and tapes; and • a folder for each participant with all relevant materials and where completed forms, papers and tapes can be stored after the session.
Post-evaluation questionnaire	We included a post-evaluation questionnaire to measure the participants' attitudes about their experience and about the website. We designed a paper and pencil questionnaire that included a Likert rating scale of ten items and an additional three open-ended items.
Determine incentives	We offered each participant a monetary incentive of $20 in addition to providing the opportunity to contribute to the design of the library website.
Arrange for a room and refreshments	We used the facilitator's office. It was equipped with a desktop computer and had enough room to accommodate the participant, the facilitator and an observer. We arranged for beverages.
Pilot the activity	We piloted the task scenarios with one or two volunteers who were not familiar with the website. We timed each task and noted any problems participants had understanding and completing the tasks. We redesigned the task scenarios to make them clear, reasonable and possible to complete within one hour.
Recruit participants	To generate a representative sample, we posted an e-mail announcement on university bulletin boards that were frequented by students and staff. The e-mail included an embedded link to a computer-based screening survey. Interested volunteers responded to the screening survey by clicking on the embedded link to the survey.
Select and schedule participants	We selected representative participants and sent an 'acceptance' letter to each with details of the sessions and scheduling information.
Reminder	The day before the session, we e-mailed each participant to remind them of the session date, time, and place.

| Prepare the room | We prepared the room the day of the sessions. The computer was set to the target website.
Each task scenario was posted on a separate letter-sized sheet of paper that was placed on a stand near the computer. All written materials were arranged in folders for each participant. The facilitator had a stopwatch, note paper and pens.
We were audio-recording, so we had plenty of tapes and backup tape recorders and batteries. Before each session we labelled the tape and other materials with the participant's number (e.g. P1), the study name, and the date.
We placed the beverages on the desk. |

Table 6.2 **Example – facilitating a think aloud protocol session**

Welcome	The facilitator welcomed each participant, introduced everyone and explained what they were about to do. The welcome was scripted to ensure that important information was communicated: • the session would be audiotaped and confidentiality would be protected in any future written and/or oral reports; • they could quit at any time without penalty; • the website was being evaluated, not the user; • they would be asked to complete tasks using the website and to think out loud about what they were doing and why; • the facilitator would not help with task completion because the session simulated how the user would complete tasks alone; • questions related to the tasks would be answered after the session. The facilitator asked the participant to read and sign the consent form, and answered questions before beginning the tasks.
Begin the activity	With the participant sitting in front of the computer, the facilitator initiated the session by reading the first scenario and posting the task sheet on a stand near the computer. The facilitator recorded the amount of time to complete the task.
Completing the tasks – observation and note-taking	The facilitator observed the participants as they completed the tasks recording difficulties, the participants' movement through the task, and their verbal comments. With a task failure, the facilitator recorded the failure and offered help so that the participant could complete the remaining activities. A similar procedure was followed with all task scenarios.
Post-evaluation questionnaire	When participants completed the task scenarios, the facilitator asked them to complete the questionnaire. We asked them to be honest with their responses, explaining that their comments would help the library to design a user-centred website. To give them more privacy, we left the room.
Conclude session	We thanked the participants for coming and distributed the incentives.
Review notes	Following each session or at the conclusion of the day, the facilitator numbered the pages and reviewed the notes of the session, inserting details and comments. We kept a running summary of notes, when possible, so that at the conclusion of all sessions, we could quickly summarise the findings. The facilitator labelled each page with the participant's number, the project name, the date and the time of the session.
Thank you	The following day we e-mailed a thank you to each participant for their contributions.

7

Communicating the findings

When you have completed the evaluation or usability test, collected and analysed the data, summarised the found issues, and determined the best recommendations for improvements to the interface, it is time to communicate the results. How you decide to present the results and the type and length of the presentation or report are dependent upon your audience, time factors and the type of evaluation activity you have completed.

Methods of communication depend on the audience, what the audience is interested in knowing, how they are best informed, and how much they want to know. The purpose of communicating the results is to determine the priority of the usability problems and how to rectify them, where in the system they occur, and how they could be addressed (Lindgaard, 1994: 103). Do not forget to consider how the report will be received, especially if people might be hurt by the findings. 'A poor reporting style can lead to hurt feelings and hostility, with the result the usability recommendations are ultimately less likely to be implemented than they would otherwise be' (Jordan, 1998: 93).

You have several options of communicating and documenting found issues in a usability study. After surveying 258 usability practitioners about the methods they use to communicate findings, Nielsen (2005) found the following:

- 42 per cent produce formal written reports;
- 36 per cent write a 'quick findings' report;
- 27 per cent have an informal meeting to discuss the findings;
- 24 per cent circulate an e-mail listing the study's top findings;
- 21 per cent have a meeting offering a formal presentation of findings;
- 15 per cent disseminate a spreadsheet listing the findings;
- 14 per cent enter usability findings into a bug-tracking database;
- 4 per cent show highlights videos from the test sessions;
- 3 per cent display posters or other physical exhibits;
- 1 per cent show a full-length video from the test sessions.

Dumas and Redish (1999: 340–1) suggest communicating the findings quickly and clearly. They offer the following suggestions:

- For people who have been involved in the duration of the activity, you may need only a short written report of findings and recommendations that are discussed in a meeting.
- For developers, managers and other readers, even if they are part of the preceding group, you may need a formal, written report that describes the methodology, participants, found issues and recommendations for improvements.

- If your development team is a client, you may need a complete and formal written report.

- When time is critical, you may want to prepare a list of findings and recommendations first and submit the complete, formal report at a later date.

- When found issues relate to the product and the development process, you may need two reports – one for the developers and another for the managers.

- To convince reluctant managers and/or developers, you may need to include a videotape illustrating the problematic issues.

- You may need to follow your organisation's policies for reporting results. This might include a 'usability bug report'.

Written reports

Written reports are produced to summarise an evaluation study and guide future work. The type and length of the report depend on the type of study and how the results will be used. This section describes formal written reports and informal written reports that summarise evaluation studies.

Formal written report

> The best usability reports are learning tools that help form a shared understanding across the team. (Jakob Nielsen, 2005)

What is a formal written report?

A formal written usability report summarises the usability study by stating clearly and simply what was done and why, how it was done, what was found, the implications and the recommendations (Gaffney, 2000e). The report summarises the study from beginning to end. It is useful as a reference for the development team during and after the project. It offers a means of obtaining agreement on the design direction and helps you deal with issues and the detail of the design problems (Hiser Group, 2006). Before writing the report, consider who will be reading the report; your objectives, i.e. the purpose of the report, what you want to accomplish; what you want your readers to do; and what you information to include (Dumas and Redish, 1999: 343; Harvey, 2003). Formal written reports, in general, include the following sections (Lindgaard, 1994: 108–10; Rubin, 1994: 290–3; Jordan, 1998: 94–6; Dumas and Redish, 1999: 349):

- *Executive summary*: In this one to two-page section, summarise the entire report by briefly describing the purpose, methods, participants, major found issues and recommendations. When writing this section consider that busy managers will read this page.

- *Table of contents*: The table of contents lists the sections and subsections that are part or the written paper or report.

- *Introduction*: This section describes the background for the evaluation method and the objectives. Include in this section the reason for conducting the test, what you hope to find, and how the findings will be used.

- *Methods*: In this section describe how you conducted the evaluation or usability testing. Describe what method you chose and why, how you recruited and selected participants, and how you collected and analysed the data. Describe the equipment and materials that you used and where you conducted the tests. The procedure describes how the sessions were conducted, the instructions, sequence of tasks, and description of the tasks. Describe the scripts or questionnaire you used and the task scenarios when relevant. Describe how the data were analysed. In general, this section should describe what you did in the study.

- *Participants*: Describe participant profiles and the demographic information in this section. Consider using a chart for the descriptive information that may include gender, age, computer expertise, and for universities and colleges, the participants' discipline and association with the university.

- *Results*: In this section describe the quantitative and qualitative summaries of the analysed data. Include such quantitative summaries as task completion rates, error rates and timing. Qualitative data can be summarised in tables, for example, how many participants said that they did not like the organisation of the website. Organise the results to be consistent with the remaining order of the findings.

- *Findings and recommendations*: In this section interpret the results into found issues explaining what the results led you to believe. Describe the problems and issues that you found and what recommendations you have for improving the website. This section is the most important part of the study. The findings should relate to the objectives of the study and the research questions. This is how the results impact the website's design and usability.

- *Other*: Include references, appendices and acknowledgments if relevant to your study.

When do you use a formal report?

Nielsen (2005) maintains that formal reports, the most common format for communicating results, although overused, are helpful in the following cases:

- *Benchmark studies or other quantitative methods*: Formal studies suffice to document and detail measurement methods and provide a benchmark for further comparisons later in the development process.

- *Competitive studies*: Formal studies are useful when testing a broad sample of alternative designs. The results are fundamental and interesting and warrant a complete report with screenshots and analysis.

- *Field studies*: Conducting studies at customer and patron locations is so rare that they warrant an archival report that can be used for years. Location studies also produce complex insights not easily explained in a quick write-up.

- *Consulting projects*: When using an expensive consultant for evaluation of the user experience, a formal report that is insightful and comprehensive is useful for future inspection.

In contrast, Wilson (1997) recommends that 'each usability evaluation should have a formal report that provides some context for the problems'. Usability reports document what the usability specialist has done, provide metrics or quantitative data that can be used as a reference point for future studies, and provide a written record of found issues. Considering both points of view, you need to decide what type of report will serve to communicate the results to your audience.

What are the advantages?

Formal written reports provide a comprehensive summary of the entire process of usability evaluation and testing. They provide a form of documentation of activities and resulting found issues that can be referred to in the future. The detailed description of methods and participants serves to validate the study, while the analysis of found issues supported with quantitative data provides support for the recommendations. Screenshots help to illustrate the problems.

Convincing reluctant team members of the value of fixing found issues is important and often difficult (Jordan, 1998: 97). A formal report provides strong evidence to support your findings and recommendations, especially when incorporating quotes from the participants.

What are the disadvantages?

Formal reports can be long, detailed and difficult to read, decreasing the likelihood that they will be read. In addition, formal reports can take much longer to complete than a quick findings report, thus delaying the development process. Therefore, to keep the work on schedule, consider submitting a quick findings report in advance of the formal report.

Informal written report

> If you can keep the report short, the developer or manager who needs to read it is more likely to tackle it soon. (Jarrett, 2004: 280)

What is an informal report?

Informal reports or quick findings reports focus on the findings and recommendations. In an informal report, briefly describe the objectives, methods and participants of the study then include a more detailed list of found issues with recommendations. A spreadsheet or chart listing the problem and recommendation(s) can be used to summarise found issues.

The objective of producing an informal report is to pass on the results as quickly as possible so that the developers or managers can complete their work. In addition, an informal report increases readability, enabling the team to move quickly to the next step in the process.

When do you use a quick informal report?'

Informal reports are often used to report on the results of usability issues found with multiple rounds of studies in an iterative design process. For example, informal reports are useful to summarise a retesting session that is conducted to check the value of design revisions.

What are the advantages?

Informal reports are completed quickly and briefly state the results, increasing the readability of the report and decreasing the time delay between the evaluation session and the report. Informal reports can be used as a quick summary before the formal report has been completed so that subsequent work is not delayed.

What are the disadvantages?

Informal reports are brief summaries that list findings and recommendations. Once design revisions have been made, the reports are no longer useful and are often discarded. Informal reports are not suitable for summarising formal usability studies which are often referred to long after the study has been completed.

Presentations

Oral presentations are necessary to successfully communicate the results of the usability evaluations. This can take place in a number of different ways. Talking informally with developers throughout the testing process is necessary to ensure reasonable and relevant recommendations as well as eliminating any surprises when you present your findings in a meeting. More formal presentations at meetings are an opportunity to share evaluation and testing information with stakeholders and the entire development team. As with other methods of communication, effective presentations are short, concentrate on action items, and show rather than tell (Jarrett, 2004: 282).

Formal presentation

What is a formal presentation?

A formal presentation, like the formal report, summarises the entire study. This type of presentation describes your methodology and participants in the study, although the focus is on the findings and recommendations.

A formal presentation of findings is enhanced when illustrated using slides or copies of screenshots and verbatim comments from participants about found issues. Video and audiotapes can be time-consuming to show, although, if you need to convince a reluctant audience, they can be helpful in further illustrating the found issue.

Before presenting your results in a formal presentation, it can helpful to engage in frequent and ongoing conversations with key members of the development team and the developers (Dumas and Redish, 1999: 341). These informal meetings help to ensure that you are all sharing similar conclusions and recommendations.

When do you use a formal presentation?

Use a formal presentation when communicating the findings of a formal usability study. For example, after completing a usability study with think aloud protocols, you can give a formal presentation to present the results to the development team or to a stakeholders group.

What are the advantages?

Formal presentations are a good way of summarising and reporting the results of a formal usability study. Formal presentations also provide a forum for the development team to discuss the recommendations and to decide on further actions.

What are the disadvantages?

Formal presentations take a little longer to prepare and present, especially if you are using video and audio-clips and presentation slides.

Informal presentation

What is an informal presentation?

Informal presentations, like the informal report, focus on the findings and recommendations. They are useful after completing an informal evaluation activity. For example, if you have completed a second series of testing after revising the website, you might use an informal presentation to talk about how the found issues were addressed and whether the actions were successful.

An informal presentation is a short, concise report that usually does not include video and audio-clips. Following the presentation, the team usually discusses the findings and recommendations, the severity of the errors and the future actions needed to address found issues.

When do you use an informal presentation?

Informal presentations are useful after completing a short evaluation activity, such as a second cycle of testing after found issues have been addressed on a website.

What are the advantages?

Informal presentations are short and concise, take little time to prepare and present, and focus on the action items. Informal presentations offer the results quickly and do not delay the development of the website.

What are the disadvantages?

Informal reports usually do not include further support (video and audio-clips or screenshots), thus the audience needs to be informed of previous evaluation activities and issues.

Appendix: Examples

E-mail request to participate

This e-mail message was posted on a university electronic bulletin board to recruit participants for a usability test.

** $20 ** University Library's Usability Test

What: Complete tasks using the new multi-resource search product

When: Morning or afternoon weekdays in April for about 30 to 60 minutes.

Where: Main Library

Why: $20 to help to create a user friendly website interface

HOW DO I SIGN UP?

Reply using the link below:

[You can insert a link to a web-based survey here.]

Contact: Gloria Librarian, glibrarian@library.su.edu, for information or questions.

WHAT WILL I DO?

You will be asked to complete a series of tasks using the multi-resource search product and to tell us what you think about using the website. The sessions will be recorded on audiotape and will take approximately 30 to 60 minutes. Your responses will be confidential.

WHAT ARE THE BENEFITS?

You will be helping the university library create a new product and get a peek at a hot new multi-resource search product. For your time and contributions you will receive $20.

WHERE?

Usability testing will be conducted in the Main Library by the library researcher, Carole Researcher (cresearcher@ library.su.edu).

WHEN?

Usability testing sessions will be scheduled in the morning or afternoon on Monday through Friday in April 2008. Other accommodations can be made, if these times are not satisfactory.

WHO IS ELIGIBLE?

We welcome students, staff, and faculty of Somewhere University.

Thank you,

Multi-Resource Search Implementation Group

Screening questionnaire

A screening questionnaire is used to select a representative sample of participants from the pool of volunteers based on their responses.

In order for us to select a diverse set of participants who are similar to our typical users, please answer the following questions by placing an X on the line near your choice or write your answer on the line.

1. Would you like to participate in the usability testing of the multi-database and resource search?
   _____ Yes
   _____ No

2. What is your name? _____

3. What is your e-mail address?_____

4. Please indicate your status.
   _____ undergraduate – 1st year
   _____ undergraduate – 2nd year
   _____ undergraduate – beyond 2nd year
   _____ graduate student
   _____ faculty
   _____ staff
   _____ other (please specify) _____

5. What is your primary affiliation?
   _____ College of Fine Arts
   _____ Heinz School of Public Policy and Management
   _____ College of Humanities and Social Sciences
   _____ Carnegie Institute of Technology
   _____ Tepper School of Business

_____ School of Computer Science
_____ Mellon College of Science
_____ Other (please specify) _____

6. Is your first language English?
_____ Yes
_____ No
_____ Other (please specify _____

Usability testing introduction

This introduction was read to each participant before beginning a think aloud protocol session.

Thank you for volunteering to participate. My name is Carole George and this is _____ (observer).

We've asked you to participate in an evaluation of this new software website interface, the screen displays, to determine how easy it is to use. Please be honest in your responses.

With your permission, I will be audiotaping your responses so that note-taking won't slow down the evaluation. All information will be confidential, and you can stop at any time without penalty.

We will complete usability testing on the [product name] software that will enable users to search multiple databases and resources with one query. Your responses will help us to make this website interface user friendly.

We will complete think aloud protocols. I will ask you to complete tasks using the software. Please verbalise what you are doing and why you are doing it.

I won't offer help because you will be using the website as

though you were at home or at work, however I will answer your questions after the session.

This is not a test of your ability to use this software, but the usability of the software; there are no right or wrong answers

Do you have any questions? Then let's begin

Facilitator's task sheet for notes

The example below shows the first scenario with three tasks. This task sheet was part of a usability testing session of a multi-database search product. Each scenario would be printed on a separate sheet. The task sheets are used for record-keeping and notes.

Participant: _____   Date: _____

TASK 1:   Time: start: _____ end: _____

Imagine that you're taking a psychology class and you need additional information about Sigmund Freud for a presentation.

Show me the full text article about Sigmund Freud.

Did the tester successfully complete the task?
_____ yes   _____ no

Show me how you would e-mail the article to yourself.

Did the tester successfully complete the task?
_____ yes   _____ no

Examine the list of found resources and select a second resource about Freud.

Did the tester successfully complete the task?

_____ yes   _____ no

Describe comments, problems.

Post-test questionnaire

The following post-test questionnaire was used following a usability study with think aloud protocols of a federated search product.

Please indicate which of the following you have used (check all that apply).

_____ Cameo (library catalogue)   _____ Library databases

_____ Multi-database search   _____ CiteSeer

_____ Google   _____ Yahoo or other

_____ Amazon.com

_____ Other searches   _____

Indicate your level of agreement by checking the column of the rating. (Check N/A if not applicable.)

The multi-database and research search:		1	2	3	4	5		N/A
Overall I am satisfied with the MetaLib search.	Strongly disagree	☐	☐	☐	☐	☐	Strongly agree	☐
It was easy to learn this system.	Strongly disagree	☐	☐	☐	☐	☐	Strongly agree	☐
The system gives me error messages that clearly tell me how to fix the problem.	Strongly disagree	☐	☐	☐	☐	☐	Strongly agree	☐
It is easy to find the information I need.	Strongly disagree	☐	☐	☐	☐	☐	Strongly agree	☐
The screen instructions are easy to understand.	Strongly disagree	☐	☐	☐	☐	☐	Strongly agree	☐
The names of links and labels are easy to understand.	Strongly disagree	☐	☐	☐	☐	☐	Strongly agree	☐
The purpose of the icons is easy to understand.	Strongly disagree	☐	☐	☐	☐	☐	Strongly agree	☐
The appearance of this system makes it appealing to use.	Strongly disagree	☐	☐	☐	☐	☐	Strongly agree	☐
If the library had training sessions, I would attend.	Strongly disagree	☐	☐	☐	☐	☐	Strongly agree	☐
I prefer to search a set with fewer databases and resources and have a shorter wait time.	Strongly disagree	☐	☐	☐	☐	☐	Strongly agree	☐

Use the back of the paper if you need more space.

What was most frustrating in this multi-database and resource search?

If you could change anything about this system what would you change?

Please add you comments or questions.

Informed consent form

The informed consent form is used to inform participants of their rights and to gain their written consent of their willingness to participate.

Somewhere University Library

Consent Form – Multi-search Usability Testing

You will be participating in a usability study to evaluate the OneQuery-MultiResource system. The results of this research will be used to improve the usability of the website. You will participate in a think aloud protocol that will take approximately 30–60 minutes and will take place in an office in Somewhere University Library. You will be asked to complete a series of tasks using the OneQuery-MultiResource system and to comment aloud about the website. Your comments will be audiotaped and a researcher and observer will take notes. You will complete a short questionnaire about the usability of the website.

The usability study will be conducted by the library researcher, Ann Researcher and will be observed by a library associate. Your participation is voluntary and if you wish to terminate participation in this study at any time, you have the right to do so without penalty.

This study is funded by [name of organisation] which is supporting the costs of this research. Neither [name of funding agency] nor [name of facilitator] will receive any financial benefit based on the results of the study.

If you have any questions about this study, please ask them now or any time throughout the study by contacting:

Ann Researcher
Human Factors Researcher
Somewhere University Library
One First Street
Phone: 555-555-5555
E-mail: Aresearcher@somewhere.edu

You may report any objections to the study either orally or in writing to:

IRB Chair
c/o Regulatory Compliance Administration
Somewhere University
One First Street
Phone: 555-555-5555
E-mail: irbchair@somewhere.edu

Although you might feel frustrated or uneasy while completing tasks, there is minimal risk to participants. A personal benefit you might get from participating is the chance to provide feedback that will affect the usability of a library product that is of benefit to the [name of university] community. As appreciation for your contributions and time, you will receive $20 in cash at the [name of office] office immediately after the session.

The results of the think aloud protocols and the questionnaire responses will be presented in reports or publications in such a way as to maintain your anonymity at all times. The audio or videotapes and data will be identified by participant identification code, not by name and will be saved for a period of two (2) years. Only the members of the research group will have access to these files.

I understand the nature of this study and agree to participate. I received a signed copy of my consent. I give [name of facilitator] and her associates permission to present this work in written and/or oral form for teaching or presentations to advance the knowledge of science and/or academia, without further permission from me provided that my image or identity is not disclosed.

Participant signature: _____

Date: _____

I understand that the researchers may want to use a short portion of any audio-recording for illustrative reasons in presentations of this work in the classroom or at professional meetings. I give my permission to do so provided that my name and face will not appear.

_____ Yes _____ No
Please initial here _____

Heuristic evaluation – reviewer's form

The heuristic evaluation reviewer form is used by reviewers to report problems or issues. When each reviewer uses a similar form, the results are reported in a consistent manner.

Evaluator: HE no.	Severity rating:
Problem:	
Evidence:	
Explanation/Describe the heuristic:	
Possible solution and /or trade-offs:	
Severity rating (0 to 4 with 0 the least severe and 4 the most severe):	
Screenshot	

Glossary

Affinity diagramming – a technique for organising concepts. Similar to brainstorming, where participants offer suggestions, comments and ideas in a free-flowing manner, with affinity diagramming each idea is written on a sticky note rather than submitted verbally. Notes are then organised by category on a large board or wall, and the resulting groups are discussed.

Attitude measure – a method of quantifying subjective ratings of attitudes and opinions. Attitudes are often measured using rating scales such as the Likert or Thurstone scale. In usability evaluation, attitude measures are used to gauge users' opinions, feelings or perceptions about the usability and design of the website or website interface.

Audiotape – a method of capturing data by audio-recording verbal discussions generated during usability evaluation sessions such as focus groups, interviews, participatory design sessions and think aloud protocols. Audiotaping captures the details of the discussion, reduces the need for note-taking, provides a record of the audio proceedings for later review, and provides further illustration for presentations to design and development groups.

Benchmark – a reference point for usability testing. Benchmarks include empirical measures such as completion rates, error rates, completion time, and attitude measures such as how users feel about the ease of use or the appearance of the user interface. In an iterative design process, benchmarks are a means of comparing system revisions over time and to indicate whether design changes have successfully addressed the issues or problems found in usability testing.

Benchmark testing – a usability testing method to measure levels of performance (completion rates, error rates, completion time and attitude measures) in order to determine measures for comparison over time. Benchmark testing is used in an iterative design process to measure the usability of a user interface and to provide points of reference to indicate whether design changes have successfully addressed the issues or problems found in usability testing.

Brainstorming – a group activity that generates a broad range of ideas, opinions, suggestions and comments. The discussion is led by a moderator who poses questions or issues statements to elicit feedback from participants. The session is spontaneous, free-flowing, and occurs in an atmosphere free from criticism. Brainstorming is most effective when criticism is held until all ideas have been presented.

Card sorting – a technique for organising concepts related to the website which is useful in the early stages of development. Participants group cards that are labelled with the concept (e.g. link names) into meaningful categories. The grouping and the discussion surrounding the reasons for the groups form the basis for revealing patterns that end-users expect to find.

Chunking information – the act of grouping information into small groups or chunks to assist the user in the mental processing of the information. Information is often presented in chunked format on websites and/or user interfaces to assist users' short-term memory and improve the readability.

Cognitive walkthrough – a usability evaluation method to find usability problems at any point in the development. Reviewers inspect the website by completing representative tasks using a prototype of the system or the completed system. As the reviewers complete the tasks, they consider how a representative user might experience the website and how difficult it is for the user to complete the tasks. Reviewers measure the usability of the website based on their understanding of a task analysis that describes what users need to do and know to complete the tasks.

Confidentiality – ensuring that the information generated in usability studies and reported in papers and/or presentations cannot be linked to individual participants. Confidentiality guarantees that the privacy of individuals will be protected and identifying information will not be released to individuals who are not directly involved in the study. A stricter form of confidentiality is anonymity, which means that the participants' identity will not be revealed in resulting papers and/or presentations and not even to the researchers. Anonymity is often associated with survey research and questionnaires.

Consistency – the degree to which the system performs in a predictable manner throughout the website (Krug, 2000: 145). Consistency in website design helps users learn how to navigate the website and creates a consistent design that supports a sense of 'place', knowing where they are in the website and how to move through the website easily. Consistency applies to many aspects of the design including page navigation, use of terminology, headings and subheadings, use of colour, page layout and design.

Content experts – in usability design and development this refers to the team members who have expert-level knowledge of the content areas presented in the website or system. In the design of library websites, the term often refers to the librarians and archivists who are knowledgeable about the library resources.

Contextual interview – a usability evaluation method that generates information using observations of representative users completing a set of predefined tasks using a prototype of the target website or the actual website. The value of contextual interviews is that the observations take place in the user's own environment.

Designers – in usability evaluation designers are responsible for conceptualising and planning the website. In user-centred design, designers focus on the user. As in many university and college libraries, designers can also be the developers who create the website.

Developers – in usability evaluation, developers are responsible for creating the website based on the designers' plan and conceptualisation. As in many university and college libraries, the designers can also be the developers who create the website.

Development team – a diverse group of specialists from fields such as content, design, development, human factors, usability, multimedia, and even target users (Rubin, 1994: 13). The team members will provide their individual perspectives throughout the design and development of a website interface and the usability evaluation and testing.

Effectiveness – the degree to which a user is able to complete tasks successfully, an indicator that the product is easy to use. Measures in usability testing that reflect effectiveness are task completion rates and error rates.

Efficiency – the degree to which users are able to consistently complete tasks successfully within a reasonable rate of time. Measures in usability testing that reflect efficiency are task completion rates, task completion time and error rates.

Empirical methods – these are based on observations and measurements and generate quantitative data. Quantitative data can be collected using methods such as think aloud protocols, surveys and attitude scales. In these methods, the data can be observed and measured, and then using a form of quantitative analysis, result in information that can be used as benchmark data for comparison over time.

End-user interface – see *user interface.*

End-users – the primary people who will use the completed system. For library websites, although users outside the school's community frequent the website, the primary end-users are the students, faculty and employees of the university or college.

Error – this occurs during usability evaluation and testing when the result of an action is not what the participant intended. For example, when using a library website, the participant may hit a navigational link that goes to an unexpected page, resulting in them having to go back and try a different link.

Evaluation – the process of assessing the value of a system in order to refine it so that it is easy-to-use and useful. To complete a usability evaluation, the evaluator collects data about usability issues, compiles and interprets the data, and communicates the findings to the development team who use the information to increase the usability and usefulness of the system.

Face-to-face – a situation where people interact with each other directly, for example, during interviews, focus groups, contextual interviews and participatory design.

Facilitator – the person who leads the usability evaluation session. Unlike the moderator, the facilitator takes an active role in the session by establishing the objectives, guiding the discussion, encouraging participants' involvement by using prompts and questions, and observing and/or commenting on behaviour and responses.

Focus group – a moderated discussion with a group of representative users or stakeholders who discuss a particular issue related to the library website design or redesign. The moderator follows a prewritten, loosely structured script to direct the conversation around the topic of interest.

Goal – the desired outcome. For the intended users of a website, the goals are their expectations. For the development team, the goals are what they expect the website to provide for users. A user-centred website focuses on the users' goals.

Heuristic evaluation – a method of evaluating the usability of a website that involves up to five expert reviewers to examine the website or end-user interface to look for usability issues as compared with a set of heuristics – widely accepted standards.

Heuristics – a set of usability standards or principles that have been accepted by experts in the field. In the case of website design and evaluation, this refers to usability engineering.

High-fidelity prototype – a working version of the final product. It is created using software, is computer-based, and functions similar to the final product. It resembles the final product closely by including design details and functionality, thus permitting realistic user interactions.

Human factors research – the study of the interaction of humans with non-human systems. In usability evaluation, it is the study the interaction of humans with computers and computer systems, for example, the website and website interface.

Human–computer interaction (HCI) – the study of how people, the users, interact with computers and computer systems, for example, the website and website interface.

Informed consent – during usability evaluation studies, the participants' rights, interests and dignity need to be protected. An informed consent form is used to fully inform participants of the procedures, risks, and their rights and confidentiality issues related to participation in the usability evaluation. Participants provide their consent in writing.

Interview – used to elicit information from participants about a broad or specific topic. The researcher poses a series of questions surrounding an issue to participants to learn more about the issue. Interviews can be conducted person-to-person or in groups (focus groups). Interviews, which either loosely or closely follow a script, can be structured, semi-structured or unstructured.

Iterative design – a cyclical process that starts early in the website's development and continues until the website end-user interface meets usability standards. It is a repeated cycle of design, evaluation, redesign and evaluation, which continues until the interface is completed. Each cycle of evaluation feeds the design of the following cycle. Depending on the depth and complexity, website development can include many rounds of design, testing and redesign.

Learnability – a characteristic of a usable website which describes the degree to which a novice user can learn how to complete basic tasks quickly and easily. Indicators of website learnability include the task completion rate, task completion time, and the number of references to documentation, help and training.

Likert scale – a rating scale frequently used in questionnaires and surveys to gauge users' attitudes, perceptions and opinions regarding an issue. Likert scales often use a five-point scale to indicate the degree to which a participant agrees or disagrees with a statement. Rating scales typically range from '1 = strongly disagree' to '5 = strongly agree'.

Low-fidelity prototype – an early, simple draft of the target website with main conceptual areas but little detail, typically a paper prototype. Low-fidelity prototypes are used in the early stages of the development to test broad design concepts.

Mock-up – another name for prototype – a draft of the end-user interface. Mock-ups usually refer to low-fidelity paper prototypes although can refer to more sophisticated draft versions of the target website.

Moderator – the coordinator of the usability evaluation group sessions. By working with the group, the moderator intervenes only when necessary to prompt discussion, but otherwise lets the participants take the lead; this contrasts with the role of the facilitator who is expected to take the lead.

Navigation – describes how easily users move through the system and understand where they are and how to return to previously viewed pages.

Non-empirical methods – are based on users' subjective perceptions, opinions and/or comments about the system or proposed system. Non-empirical usability evaluation methods include inspection methods such as heuristic evaluation and cognitive reviews and participants' subjective comments and suggestions.

Paper prototype – a draft of the proposed website created on paper. It can be as simple as a black and white hand-drawn illustration of the proposed website pages. Software can be used to create a more detailed, sophisticated draft with colour, icons, buttons and fonts.

Participant – someone who is involved in a usability evaluation activity. The participant is usually a representative user or someone from the development team.

Participatory design – sometimes referred to as participative inquiry, participatory design describes multiple methods that bring together stakeholders, most importantly representative users, to work towards developing a user-centred design. The methods of inquiry generate feedback from stakeholders regarding all aspects of website development and use (Rubin, 1994: 20).

Pilot test – an initial trial run of the evaluation technique or script to confirm that the process is well-designed. The objective of pilot testing is to search for problems with the implementation method; the clarity of the language, vocabulary and tasks; and the technology if the technique is computer-based.

Prototype – a draft copy of the interface, the pages of the proposed website. Prototypes can be developed to serve many goals – 'to discover or refine user requirements, inspire or explore design ideas, share or co-develop designs with participants, make a precise test of specific open issues, and share or deploy early implementation efforts' (Rossen and Carroll, 2001: 198).

Questionnaire – a method of surveying participants by asking them to answer questions or respond to statements about a relevant issue. Questionnaires are often administered using paper and pencil methods and distributed through the mail to groups, or directly person-to-person; or by making them available electronically.

Random sample – a method of selecting participants from the population of users. Because in most cases not all users can be included in the evaluation session, a smaller group of participants who represent the population is selected. Selecting participants in a manner that every user has an opportunity to be selected is a random sample (similar to a lottery draw). Larger random samples are generally considered to have similar attributes to the population of users.

Readability – a term used to describe the ease with which something can be read. Readability is measured by vocabulary and complexity of sentence structure. In interface development, a high degree of readability improves the usability of the website. On a user interface readability is also affected by page layout, type of font, text size and colour.

Representative sample – includes participants who have characteristics similar to the population of users regarding such things as age, gender, computer experience, and discipline or affiliation.

Response – the specific piece of information that a participant provides when taking part in an evaluation session or activity. For example, if a participant completes a questionnaire, the answer to a question is a response.

Scenario – see *task scenario.*

Screenshot – a picture of a user interface screen, also known as a screen capture or screen snap. Screenshots can be used in a participatory design session, some usability testing or in an evaluation report as a record of the user interface that was used in usability testing.

Script – a series of statements and/or questions or a set of instructions used in focus groups, participatory design sessions, interviews, scenarios and/or other evaluation sessions. It is a guide for the facilitator or moderator to follow during the sessions to keep discussions on track and/or to standardise procedures.

Selection bias – a sample of participants in an evaluation where those selected do not represent the target users. This happens frequently when participants are asked to volunteer. One method of avoiding selection bias with volunteers is to use a screening method to select a sample that is more representative of the target users.

Site visit – going to the place where people work with the target website. Site visits are used in contextual interviews to observe users operate the website in their own environment.

Stakeholder – anyone who has an interest in or is involved in the design, development and use of the website. This includes content experts, designers and developers, human factors researchers and usability specialists, and members of the target user population.

Survey – a method of collecting information by posing questions to the representative participants. The two basic categories of surveys are questionnaires and interviews, although each method has variations within the group.

Target user – see *end-user*.

Task – what the user needs to do to achieve the desired result. For example, a task might be to search for a specific book using the library website.

Task analysis – describes, in a step-by-step manner, the actions and/or cognitive processes (mental thoughts and activities) necessary to complete the tasks. A task analysis informs the design of the interface and provides a basis for developing scenarios for evaluation methods such as think aloud protocols and cognitive walkthroughs.

Task completion rate – the measure of the number of successful completions for each task. A task completion rate is calculated for each task. It can be used to help prioritise problems and measure the degree of difficulty compared with other tasks. The task completion rate can be calculated as: (number of successful completions / total number of attempts) × 100.

Task completion time – the amount of time it takes a participant to complete the task either successfully or unsuccessfully.

Task error rate – the measure of the number of errors made by participants while completing a task. A task error rate is calculated for each task. The task error rate can be used to help prioritise problems and measure the degree of difficulty compared with other tasks. The task error rate can be computed thus: (total number of errors / total number of attempts) × 100 = task error rate.

Task scenario – a realistic story that describes an activity or situation that target users might encounter when operating the system. Scenarios are often used early in the design cycle to illustrate typical users and their expectations, thus enabling the design to focus on users.

Think aloud protocol – a method employed in usability testing of the target website. In a think aloud protocol, representative users complete a series of tasks designed to simulate their real-world use of the website. During task completion, participants are encouraged to talk about their thoughts, feelings and opinions of the website.

Thurston scale – a rating scale frequently used in questionnaires and surveys to gauge users' attitudes, perceptions and opinions regarding an issue. Similar to the Likert scale, participants respond to a five-point scale (sometimes seven-point) to indicate the degree to which they agree or disagree with a statement. Rating scales typically range from '1 = strongly disagree' to '5 = strongly agree', although other ranges can be used.

Usability – describes how easy a product is to use. Usability ensures that a website 'is easy to learn, easy to use, easy to remember, error tolerant, and subjectively pleasing' (Usability Company, 2007).

Usability evaluation – employing empirical and non-empirical methods to collect data describing the usability of the website – how easy it is to learn, use, remember and recover from errors – to determine how pleasing it is to users. The data are used to further refine the website usability.

Usability inspection – describes non-empirical methods of usability evaluation. In usability inspection methods like heuristic evaluation, expert reviews and cognitive walkthroughs, experts look for usability problems by examining the interface from a user's perspective. Usability inspection methods do not involve representative users.

Usability professional – a person who is knowledgeable in usability evaluation methods, user-centred design, and who works on and advocates the usability and ease of use of systems and products. Usability professionals can concentrate solely on usability evaluation methods or can be involved in other aspects of developing user-centred systems and products. The background of usability professionals is broad and includes experience and/or education in varying fields. Many have studied in fields directly related to usability and others, through their experiences and self-learning, have become proficient in usability (Usability Professionals Association, year unknown).

Usability testing – describes empirical and non-empirical methods of measuring the usability of a website. Usability testing describes how users interact with the actual website or a working prototype. Changes made to the website based on found issues increase the website's usability. A frequently used method of usability testing is the think aloud protocol.

Usable – describes the usability of a product; how easy it is for people to complete their desired tasks with a system or product. See *usability*.

Usefulness – refers to 'how adequately the system supports the range of tasks that it was designed to support' (Lindgaard, 1994: 20). It also describes how adequately the system enables users to accomplish the tasks that they expect to complete in order to support their objectives.

User group – a subset of website users with similar characteristics taken from the entire population of target users. A user group from the population of users of a library website is students.

User interface – the link between the behind-the-scenes computer system and the user. Users interact with the user interface in order to access the information provided by the computer system. Elements of the user interface include the website pages, the screens, the text and the actionable items (links, icons, hyperlinks, etc.).

User needs analysis – a method of collecting information that describes the characteristics of target users, their goals and expectations for the system, anticipated problems or issues, and the environment in which they work. Several techniques can be used to determine user needs. They include contextual interviews, focus groups, interviews and surveys. User needs analysis is necessary to produce a user-centred design.

User task analysis – see *task analysis*.

User-centred design – focuses early and continuously on users while employing usability evaluation methods in an iterative design process to create a website that is easy for targeted users to complete their desired tasks.

User-friendly – describes the usability of a product – how easy it is to use. See *usability*.

Users – see *end-users*.

Videotaping – a method of capturing data by video-recording usability evaluation sessions such as focus groups, interviews, participatory design sessions and think aloud protocols. Videotaping captures the details of the discussion, reduces the need for note-taking, provides a video-recording of the proceedings for later review, and provides further illustration for presentations to design and development groups.

Website – the collection of web-based pages, files and documents that appear on the World Wide Web and link the system of information to users of the web. The website typically opens with a homepage that introduces the website to potential users and includes links to important pages on the website.

Website development cycle – the processes and steps required for the development of the website. The development cycle to create the website includes planning, requirements definition, design, usability evaluation and testing.

Work environment – the place in which users access the website. Work environment includes physical, cultural and chemical factors that surround the person in the environment. It can be an office, home, computer lab or the library.

Bibliography

Baily, B. (2005) 'Paper prototypes work as well as software prototypes', available at: *http://www.usability.gov/pubs/062005news.html* (accessed 28 January 2008).

Barnum, C. M. (2002) *Usability Testing and Research*, New York: Longman.

Barribeau, P., Butler, B., Corney, J., Doney, M., Gault, J., Gordon, J., Fetzer, R., Klein, A., Ackerson Rogers, C., Stein, I. F., Steiner, C., Urschel, H., Waggoner, T. and Palmquist, M. (2005) 'Survey research', available at: *http://writing.colostate.edu/guides/research/survey/* (accessed 28 January 2008).

Beyer, H. and Holtzblatt, K. (1998) *Contextual Design: Defining Customer-Centered Systems*, San Francisco, CA: Morgan Kaufmann.

Booth, P. A. (1989) *An Introduction to Human-Computer Interaction*, London: Lawrence Erlbaum.

Brinck, T., Gergle, D. and Wood, S. D. (2002) *Usability for the Web: Designing Websites that Work*, San Francisco, CA: Morgan Kaufmann.

Carey, D. (2007) 'Totally wired!' *Parade*, 18 November, available at: *http://www.parade.com/articles/editions/2007/edition_11-18-2007/Drew_Carey* (accessed 28 January 2008).

CustomInsight (year unknown) 'Random sampling overview', available at: *http://www.custominsight .com/articles/random-sampling.asp* (accessed 28 January 2008).

Danino, N. (2001) 'Heuristic evaluation – A step by step guide', available at: *http://www.sitepoint.com/article/ heuristic-evaluation-guide* (accessed 28 January 2008).

Dumas, J. S. and Redish, J. C. (1999) *A Practical Guide to Usability Testing*, Exeter: Intellect Ltd.

Ericsson, K. A. and Simon, H. A. (1984) *Protocol Analysis*, Cambridge, MA: MIT Press.

Ericsson, K. A. and Simon, H. A. (1993) *Protocol Analysis* (revised edn), Cambridge, MA: MIT Press.

Evaluation for Learning (1999) 'Focus groups: Part I the basics', available at: *http://www.wmich.edu/evalctr/ eval_nsltr/fall_99.htm (accessed 28 January 2008).*

Evaluation for Learning (2000) 'Focus groups: Part II the art of the moderator', available at: *http://www.wmich .edu/evalctr/eval_nsltr/winter_00.htm* (accessed 28 January 2008).

Gaffney, G. (2000a) 'What is facilitation?' available at: *http://www.infodesign.com.au/usabilityresources/general/ facilitationtechniques.asp* (accessed 28 January 2008).

Gaffney, G. (2000b) 'What is a participatory design workshop?' available at: *http://www.infodesign.com.au/ usabilityresources/design/participatorydesign.asp* (accessed 28 January 2008).

Gaffney, G. (2000c). 'What is affinity diagramming?' available at: *http://www.infodesign.com.au/ usabilityresources/general/affinitydiagramming.asp* (accessed 28 January 2008).

Gaffney, G. (2000d) 'What is a cognitive interview?' available at: *http://www.infodesign.com.au/ usabilityresources/evaluation/conductingwalkthroughs.asp* (accessed 28 January 2008).

Gaffney, G. (2000e) 'Writing usability reports'. available at: *http://www.infodesign.com.au/usabilityresources/general/ writingusabilityreports.asp* (accessed 28 January 2008).

George, C. A. (2006) *MetaLib 1 Usability Report v2*, Pittsburgh, PA: Carnegie Mellon University Libraries.

Gould, J. D. and Clayton L. (1985) 'Designing for usability: Key principles and what designers think', *Communications of the ACM* 28(3): 300–11.

Hackos, J. T. and Redish J. C. (1998) *User and Task Analysis for Interface Design*, New York: Wiley.

Hakim, J. and Spitzer, T. (2000) 'Effective prototyping for usability', paper presented at the 2000 Joint IEEE International and 18th Annual Conference on Computer Documentation Cambridge, MA, 24 September, available at: *http://ieeexplore.ieee.org/iel5/7114/19161/00887255 .pdf?isnumber=19161&prod=CNF&arnumber=887255 &arSt=&ared=&arAuthor=* (accessed 28 January 2008).

Harvey, M. (2003) *The Nuts and Bolts of College Writing*, Indianapolis, IN: Hackett Publishing.

Hiser Group (2006) 'Findings report', available at: *http://www.hiser.com.au/documentation/findings_report. .html* (accessed 28 January 2008).

Information Services and Technology (year unknown) 'Card sorting exercise: information for volunteers', available at: *http://web.mit.edu/is/usability/card-sort-instrucs.html* (accessed 28 January 2008).

Instructional Assessment Resources (IAR) (2007) 'Assess technology: survey', available at: *http://www.utexas.edu/ academic/diia/assessment/iar/tech/plan/method/survey.ph p* (accessed 28 January 2008).

Jarrett, C. (2004) 'Better reports: how to communicate the results of usability testing', paper presented at the 51st Annual Conference of the Society for Technical

Communication, Baltimore, MD, 9–12 May, available at: *http://www.stc.org/ConfProceed/2004/PDFs/0060.pdf* (accessed 28 January 2008).

Jordan, P. W. (1994) 'Methods for user interface performance measurement', in E. J. Lovesey (ed.) *Contemporary Ergonomics*, London: Taylor & Francis, pp. 451–60.

Jordan, P. W. (1998) *An Introduction to Usability*, London: Taylor & Francis.

Kasunic, M. (2005) 'Designing an effective survey', available at: *http://www.sei.cmu.edu/pub/documents/05.reports/pdf/05hb004.pdf* (accessed 28 January 2008).

Kneifel, A. A. and Guerrero, C. (2003) 'Using participative inquiry in usability analysis to align a development team's mental model with its users' needs', paper presented at STC's 50th Annual Conference, Dallas, TX, 18–21 May, available at: *http://www.stc.org/ConfProceed/2003/PDFs/STC50-092.pdf* (accessed 28 January 2008)

Krug, S. (2000) *Don't Make Me Think! A Common Sense Approach to Web Usability*, Indianapolis, IA: New Riders Publishing.

Lindgaard, G. (1994) *Usability Testing and System Evaluation: A Guide for Designing Useful Computing Systems*, Boca Raton, FL: Chapman & Hall.

Mark Boulton Design (year unknown: a) 'Card sorting. Part 2 – Facilitation', available at: *http://www.markboulton.co.uk/articles/detail/card_sorting_part_2/* (accessed 28 January 2008).

Mark Boulton Design (year unknown: b) 'Card sorting Part 3 – Analysis and reporting', available at: *http://www.markboulton.co.uk/articles/detail/card_sorting_part_3/* (accessed 28 January 2008).

Maurer, D. and Warfel, T. (2004) 'Card sorting: a definitive guide', available at: *http://www.boxesandarrows.com/*

view/card_sorting_a_definitive_guide (accessed 28 January 2008).

Mayhew, D. J. (1999) *The Usability Engineering Lifecycle: A Practitioner's Handbook for User Interface Design*, San Francisco, CA: Morgan Kaufmann.

Molich, R. and Nielsen, J. (1990) 'Improving a human-computer dialogue', *Communications of the ACM 33*(3): 338–48.

Moore, G. A. (1991) *Crossing the Chasm: Marketing and Selling High-Tech Products to Mainstream Customers*, New York: HarperCollins.

Newman, M. W. and Landay J. A. (2000) 'Sitemaps, storyboards, and specifications: A sketch of website design practice', paper presented at the 3rd Conference on Designing Interactive Systems: Processes, Practices, Methods, and Techniques, New York, 17–19 August, available at: *http://delivery.acm.org/10.1145/350000/ 347758/p263-newman.pdf?key1=347758&key2= 1003171021&coll=GUIDE&dl=GUIDE&CFID=52515 657&CFTOKEN=32776622* (accessed 28 January 2008).

Nielsen, J. (year unknown) 'Severity ratings for usability problems', available at: *http://www.useit.com/papers/ heuristic/severityrating.html* (accessed 28 January 2008).

Nielsen, J. (1992) 'The usability engineering life cycle', *IEEE Computer 25*(3): 12–22.

Nielsen, J. (1993) *Usability Engineering*, Amsterdam: Morgan Kaufmann.

Nielsen, J. (1994a) 'Enhancing the explanatory power of usability heuristics', paper presented at the ACM CHI'94 Conference, Boston, MA, 24–28 April, available at: *http://delivery.acm.org/10.1145/200000/191729/p152-nielsen.pdf?key1=191729&key2=8296337021&coll=G UIDE&dl=GUIDE&CFID=62375099&CFTOKEN=22*

178065 (accessed 28 January 2008).

Nielsen, J. (1994b) 'Guerrilla HCI: Using discount usability engineering to penetrate the intimidation barrier', available at: *http://www.useit.com/papers/guerrilla_ hci.html* (accessed 28 January 2008).

Nielsen, J. (1995) 'Using paper prototypes in home-page design'. *IEEE Software* 12(4): 88–9, 97, available at: *http://ieeexplore.ieee.org/iel1/52/8878/00391840.pdf? arnumber=391840* (accessed 28 January 2008).

Nielsen, J. (1997) 'The use and misuse of focus groups', available at: *http://www.useit.com/papers/ focusgroups.html* (accessed 28 January 2008).

Neilsen, J. (2000) *Designing Web Usability*, Indianapolis, IA: New Riders.

Nielsen, J. (2001a) 'Is navigation useful?' available at: *http://www.useit.com/alertbox/20000109.html* (accessed 28 January 2008).

Nielsen, J. (2001b) 'First rule of usability? Don't listen to users', available at: *http://www.useit.com/alertbox/ 20010805.html* (accessed 28 January 2008).

Nielsen, J. (2003a) 'Usability 101: Introduction to usability', available at: *http://www.useit.com/alertbox/ 20030825.html* (accessed 28 January 2008).

Nielsen, J. (2003b) 'Paper prototyping: getting user data before you code', available at: *http://www.useit.com/ alertbox/20030414.html* (accessed 28 January 2008).

Nielsen, J. (2005) 'Formal usability reports vs quick findings', available at: *http://www.useit.com/alertbox/ 20050425.html* (accessed 28 January 2008).

Nielsen, J. and Molich, R. (1990) 'Heuristic evaluation of user interfaces', paper presented at the ACM CHI'90 Conference, Seattle, WA, 1–5 April, available at: *http://delivery.acm.org/10.1145/100000/97281/p249- nielsen.pdf?key1=97281&key2=6507337021&coll=GUI*

DE&dl=GUIDE&CFID=62374218&CFTOKEN=6085 2484 (accessed 28 January 2008).

Norman, D. (1998) *The Invisible Computer*, Cambridge MA: MIT Press.

Robertson, J. (2001) 'Information design using card sorting', available at: *http://www.steptwo.com.au/papers/cardsorting/index.html* (accessed 28 January 2008).

Rosson, M. B. and Carroll, J. M. (2001) *Usability Engineering: Scenario-Based Development of Human Computer Interaction*, San Francisco, CA: Morgan Kaufmann.

Rubin, J. (1994) *Handbook of Usability Testing: How to Plan, Design, and Conduct Effective Tests*, New York: Wiley.

Rudd, J., Stern, K. and Isensee, S. (1996) 'Low vs high fidelity prototyping debate', *Interactions* 3(1): 76–85.

SAP Design Guild (2004) 'Using prototypes', available at: *http://www.sapdesignguild.org/resources/prototypes.asp* (accessed 28 January 2008)

Sefelin, R., Tscheligi, M. and Giller, V. (2003) 'Paper prototyping – What is it good for? A comparison of paper- and computer-based low-fidelity prototyping', paper presented at the Conference on Human Factors in Computing Systems, Ft. Lauderdale, FL, 5–10 April, available at: *http://delivery.acm.org/ 10.1145/770000/ 765986/p778-sefelin.pdf?key1=765986&key2= 9028071021&coll= GUIDE&dl=GUIDE&CFID= 52505616&CFTOKEN=75395182* (accessed 28 January 2008).

Shneiderman, B. (1997) *Designing the User Interface: Strategies for Effective Human-Computer Interaction*, Reading, MA: Addison-Wesley.

Simon, H. A. (1957) *Models of Man: Social and Rational*,

New York: John Wiley and Sons.

Snyder, C. (2001) 'Paper prototyping. IBM developer works', available at: *http://www.snyderconsulting. net/article_paperprototyping.htm* (accessed 28 January 2008).

Snyder, C. (2003) *Paper Prototyping: The Fast and Easy Way to Design and Refine User Interfaces*, San Francisco, CA: Morgan Kaufmann.

StatPac (year unknown) 'Questionnaire design; general considerations', available at: *http://www.statpac.com/ surveys/questionnaire-design.htm* (accessed 28 January 2008).

Tec-Ed Services (2008a) 'Usability testing', available at: *http://www.teced.com/services_usability_testing.html* (accessed 28 January 2008).

Tec-Ed Services (2008b) 'Field research', available at: *http://www.teced.com/services_usability_field_detail.html* (accessed 28 January 2008).

Tec-Ed Services (2008c) 'Card sorting', available at: *http://www.teced.com/services_ia_sorting.html* (accessed 28 January 2008).

Torres, R. J. (2002) *Practitioner's Handbook for User Interface Design and Development*, Upper Saddle River, NJ: Prentice Hall.

Treu, S. (1994) *User Interface Evaluation: A Structured Approach*, New York: Plenum Press.

Trochim, W. M. K. (2000) *Research Methods Knowledge Base* (2nd edn), Cincinnati, OH: Atomic Dog Publishing.

Usability BoK. 'Usability body of knowledge: Glossary. The Usability Professionals Association', available at: *http://www.usabilitybok.org/glossary* (accessed 28 January 2008).

Usability Company (2007) 'Glossary', available at: *http://www.theusabilitycompany.com/resources/glossary.*

html (accessed 28 January 2008).

Usability First (2005) 'Glossary', available at: *http://www.usabilityfirst.com/glossary/* (accessed 28 January 2008).

Usability Net (2006a) 'Focus groups', available at: *http://www.usabilitynet.org/tools/focusgroups.htm* (accessed 28 January 2008).

Usability Net (2006b) 'Affinity diagramming', available at: *http://www.usabilitynet.org/tools/affinity.htm* (accessed 28 January 2008).

Usability Net (2006c) 'Card sorting', available at: *http://www.usabilitynet.org/tools/cardsorting.htm* (accessed 28 January 2008).

Usability Net (2006d) 'Paper prototyping', available at: *http://www.usabilitynet.org/tools/prototyping.htm* (accessed 28 January 2008).

Usability Professionals Association (year unknown) 'Resources in usability', available at: *http://www.upassoc .org/usability_resources/about_usability/about_usability_ professionals.html* (accessed 28 January 2008).

Usability.gov. (year unknown: a) 'Determine website requirements', available at: *http://www.usability .gov/design/requirements.html* (accessed 28 January 2008).

Usability.gov. (year unknown: b) 'Contextual interviews', available at: *http://www.usability.gov/methods/ contextual.html* (accessed 28 January 2008).

Usability.gov. (year unknown: c) 'Perform card sorting', available at: *http://www.usability.gov/design/ cardsort.html* (accessed 28 January 2008).

Usability.gov. (year unknown: d) 'Develop a prototype', available at: *http://www.usability.gov/design/ prototyping.html* (accessed 28 January 2008).

Virzi, R. A., Sokolov, J. L. and Karis, D. (1996) 'Usability problem identification using both low- and high-fidelity prototypes', paper presented at the Conference on Human Factors in Computing Systems, Vancouver, BC, 13–18 April, available at: *http://delivery.acm .org/10.1145/240000/238516/p236-virzi.pdf?key1= 238516&key2=2050171021&coll=portal&dl=ACM&C FID=52511067&CFTOKEN=17814692* (accessed 28 January 2008).

Webcredible (year unknown) 'Focus groups', available at: *http://www.webcredible.co.uk/services/focus-groups .shtml* (accessed 28 January 2008).

Wharton, C., Rieman, J., Lewis, C. and Polson, P. (1994) 'The cognitive walkthrough method: a practitioner's guide', in Jakob Nielsen and Robert L. Mack (eds) *Usability Inspection Methods*, New York: John Wiley & Sons, pp. 105–40.

Wilson, C. (1997) 'Techniques for analyzing and reporting usability data', available at: *http://www.stcsig.org/ usability/newsletter/9710-analyzing-data.html* (accessed 28 January 2008).

Woodson, W. E. (1981) *Human Factors Design Handbook*, New York: McGraw-Hill Education.

Index

Printed in the United States
124855LV00002B/122/P

BIBLIO RPL Ltée

G - NOV. 2008